A Spiritual Canticle of the Soul
and
the Bridegroom Christ
By St. John of the Cross
Translated by David Lewis
Edited by Anthony Uyl

Devoted Publishing
Woodstock, Ontario, 2016

A Spiritual Canticle of the Soul and the Bridegroom Christ
A Spiritual Canticle of the Soul and the Bridegroom Christ
By St. John of the Cross
Translated by David Lewis
With Corrections and an Introduction by Benedict Zimmerman, O.C.D.
Edited by Anthony Uyl

Prior of St. Luke's, Wincanton, June 28, 1909

The text of A Spiritual Canticle of the Soul and the Bridegroom Christ is all in the Public Domain. This edition is published by Devoted Publishing a division of 2165467 Ontario Inc.

What kind of philosophies do you have?
Let us know!

Contact us at: devotedpub@hotmail.com
Visit us on Facebook: Devoted Publishing
Get more products via our website: www.devotedpublishing.com

Published in Woodstock, Ontario, Canada 2016.

For bulk educational rates, please contact us at the above email address.

ISBN: 978-1-988297-13-2

Table of Contents

INTRODUCTION	5
Footnotes:	8
A SPIRITUAL CANTICLE OF THE SOUL AND THE BRIDEGROOM CHRIST	9
PROLOGUE	9
Footnotes:	10
SONG OF THE SOUL AND THE BRIDEGROOM	11
ARGUMENT	17
EXPLANATION OF THE STANZAS	17
Footnotes:	17
STANZA I	18
Footnotes:	22
STANZA II	23
Footnotes:	24
STANZA III	26
Footnotes:	28
STANZA IV	29
Footnotes:	30
STANZA V	31
Footnotes:	32
STANZA VI	33
STANZA VII	35
Footnotes:	36
STANZA VIII	37
Footnotes:	38
STANZA IX	39
Footnotes:	40
STANZA X	41
Footnotes:	42
STANZA XI	43
Footnotes:	45
STANZA XII	47
Footnotes:	49
STANZA XIII	50
Footnotes:	53
STANZAS XIV, XV	54
Footnotes:	58
STANZA XV	59
Footnotes:	61
STANZA XVI	62
Footnotes:	64
STANZA XVII	65
Footnotes:	67
STANZA XVIII	68
Footnotes:	69
STANZA XIX	70
Footnotes:	71
STANZAS XX, XXI	72
Footnotes:	75
STANZA XXII	76
Footnotes:	78
STANZA XXIII	79
Footnotes:	80
STANZA XXIV	81
Footnotes:	83
STANZA XXV	84
Footnotes:	86
STANZA XXVI	87
Footnotes:	90
STANZA XXVII	91
Footnotes:	92
STANZA XXVIII	93
Footnotes:	95
STANZA XXIX	96
Footnotes:	97
STANZA XXX	98
Footnotes:	100
STANZA XXXI	101
Footnotes:	102
STANZA XXXII	103
Footnotes:	104
STANZA XXXIII	105
Footnotes:	106
STANZA XXXIV	107
Footnotes:	108
STANZA XXXV	109
Footnotes:	110
STANZA XXXVI	111
Footnotes:	113

A Spiritual Canticle of the Soul and the Bridegroom Christ

STANZA XXXVII 114	STANZA XXXIX 119
Footnotes: 115	Footnotes: 122
STANZA XXXVIII 116	STANZA XL 123
Footnotes: 118	Footnotes: 124

INTRODUCTION

THE present volume of the works of St. John of the Cross contains the explanation of the "Spiritual Canticle of the Soul and the Bridegroom Christ." The two earlier works, the "Ascent of Mount Carmel" and the "Dark Night of the Soul," dealt with the cleansing of the soul, the unremitting war against even the smallest imperfections standing in the way of union with God; imperfections which must be removed, partly by strict self-discipline, partly by the direct intervention of God, Who, searching "the reins and hearts" by means of heavy interior and exterior trials, purges away whatever is displeasing to Him. Although some stanzas refer to this preliminary state, the chief object of the "Spiritual Canticle" is to picture under the Biblical simile of Espousals and Matrimony the blessedness of a soul that has arrived at union with God.

The Canticle was composed during the long imprisonment St. John underwent at Toledo from the beginning of December 1577 till the middle of August of the following year. Being one of the principal supporters of the Reform of St. Teresa, he was also one of the victims of the war waged against her work by the Superiors of the old branch of the Order. St. John's prison was a narrow, stifling cell, with no window, but only a small loophole through which a ray of light entered for a short time of the day, just long enough to enable him to say his office, but affording little facility for reading or writing. However, St. John stood in no need of books. Having for many years meditated on every word of Holy Scripture, the Word of God was deeply written in his heart, supplying abundant food for conversation with God during the whole period of his imprisonment. From time to time he poured forth his soul in poetry; afterwards he communicated his verses to friends.

One of these poetical works, the fruit of his imprisonment, was the "Spiritual Canticle," which, as the reader will notice, is an abridged paraphrase of the Canticle of Canticles, the Song of Solomon, wherein under the image of passionate love are described the mystical sufferings and longings of a soul enamored with God.

From the earliest times the Fathers and Doctors of the Church had recognized the mystical character of the Canticle, and the Church had largely utilized it in her liturgy. But as there is nothing so holy but that it may be abused, the Canticle almost more than any other portion of Holy Scripture, had been misinterpreted by a false Mysticism, such as was rampant in the middle of the sixteenth century. It had come to pass, said the learned and saintly Augustinian, Fray Luis de Leon, that that which was given as a medicine was turned into poison, [1] so that the Ecclesiastical authority, by the Index of 1559, forbade the circulation of the Bible or parts of the Bible in any but the original languages, Hebrew, Greek, and Latin; and no one knew better than Luis de Leon himself how rigorously these rules were enforced, for he had to expiate by nearly five years' imprisonment the audacity of having translated into Castilian the Canticle of Canticles. [2]

Again, one of the confessors of St. Teresa, commonly thought to have been the Dominican, Fray Diego de Yanguas, on learning that the Saint had written a book on the Canticle, ordered her to throw it into the fire, so that we now only possess a few fragments of her work, which, unknown to St. Teresa, had been copied by a nun.

It will now be understood that St. John's poetical paraphrase of the Canticle must have been welcome to many contemplative souls who desired to kindle their devotion with the words of Solomon, but were unable to read them in Latin. Yet the text alone, without explanation, would have helped them little; and as no one was better qualified than the author to throw light on the mysteries hidden under oriental imagery, the Venerable Ann of Jesus, Prioress of the Carmelite convent at Granada, requested St. John to write a commentary on his verses. [3] He at first excused himself, saying that he was no longer in that state of spiritual exuberance in which he had been when composing the Canticle, and that there only remained to him a confused recollection of the wonderful operations of Divine grace during the period of his imprisonment. Ann of Jesus was not satisfied with this answer; she not only knew that St. John had lost nothing of his fervor, though he might no longer experience the same feelings, but she remembered what had happened to St. Teresa under similar circumstances, and believed the same thing might happen to St. John. When St. Teresa was obliged to write on some mystical phenomena, the nature of which she did not fully understand, or whose effect she had forgotten, God granted her unexpectedly a repetition of her former experiences so as to enable her to fully study the matter and report on it. [4] Venerable Ann of Jesus felt sure that if St. John undertook to write an explanation of the

A Spiritual Canticle of the Soul and the Bridegroom Christ
Canticle he would soon find himself in the same mental attitude as when he composed it.

St. John at last consented, and wrote the work now before us. The following letter, which has lately come to light, gives some valuable information of its composition. The writer, Magdalen of the Holy Spirit, nun of Veas, where she was professed on August 6, 1577, was intimately acquainted with the Saint.

"When the holy father escaped from prison, he took with him a book of poetry he had written while there, containing the verses commencing In the beginning was the Word,' and those others: I know the fountain well which flows and runs, though it is night,' and the canticle, Where have you hidden yourself?' as far as O nymphs of Judea' (stanza XVIII.). The remaining verses he composed later on while rector of the college of Baeza (15791 - 81), while some of the explanations were written at Veas at the request of the nuns, and others at Granada. The Saint wrote this book in prison and afterwards left it at Veas, where it was handed to me to make some copies of it. Later on it was taken away from my cell, and I never knew who took it. I was much struck with the vividness and the beauty and subtlety of the words. One day I asked the Saint whether God had given him these words which so admirably explain those mysteries, and He answered: Child, sometimes God gave them to me, and at other times I sought them myself.'" [5]

The autograph of St. John's work which is preserved at Jaén bears the following title:

"Explanation of Stanzas treating of the exercise of love between the soul and Jesus Christ its Spouse, dealing with and commenting on certain points and effects of prayer; written at the request of Mother Ann of Jesus, prioress of the Discalced Carmelite nuns of St. Joseph's convent, Granada, 1584."

As might be expected, the author dedicated the book to Ann of Jesus, at whose request he had written it. Thus, he began his Prologue with the following words: "Inasmuch as this canticle, Reverend Mother (Religiosa Madre), seems to have been written," etc. A little further on he said: "The stanzas that follow, having been written under the influence of that love which proceeds from the overflowing mystical intelligence, cannot be fully explained. Indeed, I do not purpose any such thing, for my sole purpose is to throw some general light over them, since Your Reverence has asked me to do so, and since this, in my opinion too, is the better course." And again: "I shall, however, pass over the more ordinary (effects of prayer), and treat briefly of the more extraordinary to which they are subject who, by the mercy of God, have advanced beyond the state of beginners. This I do for two reasons: the first is that much is already written concerning beginners; and the second is that I am addressing myself to Your Reverence at your own bidding; for you have received from Our Lord the grace of being led on from the elementary state and led inwards to the bosom of His divine love." He continues thus: "I therefore trust, though I may discuss some points of scholastic theology relating to the interior commerce of the soul with God, that I am not using such language altogether in vain, and that it will be found profitable for pure spirituality. For though Your Reverence is ignorant of scholastic theology, you are by no means ignorant of mystical theology, the science of love, etc."

From these passages it appears quite clearly that the Saint wrote the book for Venerable Ann of Jesus and the nuns of her convent. With the exception of an edition published at Brussels in 1627, these personal allusions have disappeared from both the Spanish text and the translations, [6] nor are they to be found in Mr. Lewis's version. There cannot be the least doubt that they represent St. John's own intention, for they are to be found in his original manuscript. This, containing, in several parts, besides the Explanation of the Spiritual Canticle, various poems by the Saint, was given by him to Ann of Jesus, who in her turn committed it to the care of one of her nuns, Isabelle of the Incarnation, who took it with her to Baeza, where she remained eleven years, and afterwards to Jaén, where she founded a convent of which she became the first prioress. She there caused the precious manuscript to be bound in red velvet with silver clasps and gilt edges. It still was there in 1876, and, for all we know, remains to the present day in the keeping of the said convent. It is a pity that no photographic edition of the writings of St. John (so far as the originals are preserved) has yet been attempted, for there is need for a critical edition of his works.

The following is the division of the work: Stanzas I. to IV. are introductory; V. to XII. refer to the contemplative life in its earlier stages; XIII. to XXI., dealing with what the Saint calls the Espousals, appertain to the Unitive way, where the soul is frequently, but not habitually, admitted to a transient union with God; and XXII. to the end describe what he calls Matrimony, the highest perfection a soul can attain this side of the grave. The reader will find an epitome of the whole system of mystical theology in the explanation of Stanza XXVI.

This work differs in many respects from the "Ascent" and the "Dark Night." Whereas these are strictly systematic, preceding on the line of relentless logic, the "Spiritual Canticle," as a poetical work ought to do, soars high above the divisions and distinctions of the scholastic method. With a boldness akin to that of his Patron Saint, the Evangelist, St. John rises to the highest heights, touching on a subject that should only be handled by a Saint, and which the reader, were he a Saint himself, will do

St. John of the Cross

well to treat cautiously: the partaking by the human soul of the Divine Nature, or, as St. John calls it, the Deification of the soul (Stanza XXVI. sqq.), These are regions where the ordinary mind threatens to turn; but St. John, with the knowledge of what he himself had experienced, not once but many times, what he had observed in others, and what, above all, he had read of in Holy Scripture, does not shrink from lifting the veil more completely than probably any Catholic writer on mystical theology has done. To pass in silence the last wonders of God's love for fear of being misunderstood, would have been tantamount to ignoring the very end for which souls are led along the way of perfection; to reveal these mysteries in human language, and say all that can be said with not a word too much, not an uncertain or misleading line in the picture: this could only have been accomplished by one whom the Church has already declared to have been taught by God Himself (divinitus instructus), and whose books She tells us are filled with heavenly wisdom (coelesti sapientia refertos). It is hoped that sooner or later She will proclaim him (what many grave authorities think him to be) a Doctor of the Church, namely, the Doctor of Mystical theology. [7]

As has already been noticed in the Introduction to the "Ascent," the whole of the teaching of St. John is directly derived from Holy Scripture and from the psychological principles of St. Thomas Aquinas. There is no trace to be found of an influence of the Mystics of the Middle Age, with whose writings St. John does not appear to have been acquainted. But throughout this treatise there are many obvious allusions to the writings of St. Teresa, nor will the reader fail to notice the encouraging remark about the publication of her works (stanza xiii, sect. 8). The fact is that the same Venerable Ann of Jesus who was responsible for the composition of St. John's treatise was at the same time making preparations for the edition of St. Teresa's works which a few years later appeared at Salamanca under the editorship of Fray Luis de Leon, already mentioned.

Those of his readers who have been struck with, not to say frightened by, the exactions of St. John in the "Ascent" and the "Dark Night," where he demands complete renunciation of every kind of satisfaction and pleasure, however legitimate in themselves, and an entire mortification of the senses as well as the faculties and powers of the soul, and who have been wondering at his self-abnegation which caused him not only to accept, but even to court contempt, will find here the clue to this almost inhuman attitude. In his response to the question of Our Lord, "What shall I give you for all you have done and suffered for Me?" "Lord, to suffer and be despised for You" -- he was not animated by grim misanthropy or stoic indifference, but he had learned that in proportion as the human heart is emptied of Self, after having been emptied of all created things, it is open to the influx of Divine grace. This he fully proves in the "Spiritual Canticle." To be made "partaker of the Divine Nature," as St. Peter says, human nature must undergo a radical transformation. Those who earnestly study the teaching of St. John in his earlier treatises and endeavor to put his recommendations into practice, will see in this and the next volume an unexpected perspective opening before their eyes, and they will begin to understand how it is that the sufferings of this time -- whether voluntary or involuntary -- are not worthy to be compared with the glory to come that shall be revealed in us.

Mr. Lewis's masterly translation of the works of St. John of the Cross appeared in 1864 under the auspices of Cardinal Wiseman. In the second edition, of 1889, he made numerous changes, without, however, leaving a record of the principles that guided him. Sometimes, indeed, the revised edition is terser than the first, but just as often the old one seems clearer. It is more difficult to understand the reasons that led him to alter very extensively the text of quotations from Holy Scripture. In the first edition he had nearly always strictly adhered to the Douay version, which is the one in official use in the Catholic Church in English-speaking countries. It may not always be as perfect as one would wish it to be, but it must be acknowledged that the wholesale alteration in Mr. Lewis's second edition is, to say the least, puzzling. Even the Stanzas have undergone many changes in the second edition, and it will be noticed that there are some variants in their text as set forth at the beginning of the book, and as repeated at the heading of each chapter.

The present edition, allowing for some slight corrections, is a reprint of that of 1889.

Benedict Zimmerman, Prior, O.C.D.
St. Lukes, Wincanton, Somerset,
Feast of St. Simon Stock,
May 16, 1909.

A Spiritual Canticle of the Soul and the Bridegroom Christ

Footnotes:

1. Los nombres de Cristo.' Introduction.
2. This exceptionally severe legislation, justified by the dangers of the time, only held good for Spain and the Spanish colonies, and has long since been revised. It did not include the Epistles and Gospels, Psalms, Passion, and other parts of the daily service.
3. Ann de Lobera, born at Medina del Campo, November 25, 1545, was a deaf-mute until her eighth year. When she applied for admission to the Carmelite convent at Avila St. Teresa promised to receive her not so much as a novice, but as her companion and future successor; she took the habit August 1, 1570, and made her profession at Salamanca, October 21, 1571. She became the first prioress of Veas, and was entrusted by St. Teresa with the foundation of Granada (January 1582), where she found St. John of the Cross, who was prior of the convent of The Martyrs (well known to visitors of the Alhambra although no longer a convent). St. John not only became the director and confessor of the convent of nuns, but remained the most faithful helper and the staunchest friend of Mother Ann throughout the heavy trials which marred many years of her life. In 1604 she went to Paris, to found the first convent of her Order in France, and in 1607 she proceeded to Brussels, where she remained until her death, March 4, 1621, The heroic nature of her virtues having been acknowledged, she was declared Venerable' in 1878, and it is hoped that she will soon be beatified.
4. See Life of St. Teresa': ed. Baker (London, 1904), ch. xiv. 12, xvi. 2, xviii. 10.
5. Manuel Serrano y Sanz,' Apuntos para una Biblioteca de Escritores españoles. (1903, p. 399).
6. Cf. Berthold-Ignace de Sainte Anne, Vie de la Mère Anne de Jésui' (Malines, 1876), I. 343 ff.
7. On this subject see Fray Eulogio de San José, Doctorado de Santa Teresa de Jesús y de San Juan de la Cruz.' Córdoba, 1896.

St. John of the Cross

A SPIRITUAL CANTICLE OF THE SOUL AND THE BRIDEGROOM CHRIST [8]

PROLOGUE

INASMUCH as this canticle seems to have been written with some fervor of love of God, whose wisdom and love are, as is said in the book of Wisdom, [9] so vast that they reach "from end to end," and as the soul, taught and moved by Him, manifests the same abundance and strength in the words it uses, I do not purpose here to set forth all that greatness and fullness the spirit of love, which is fruitful, embodies in it. Yes, rather it would be foolishness to think that the language of love and the mystical intelligence -- and that is what these stanzas are -- can be at all explained in words of any kind, for the Spirit of our Lord who helps our weakness -- as St. Paul says [10] -- dwelling in us makes petitions for us with groaning unutterable for that which we cannot well understand or grasp so as to be able to make it known. "The Spirit helps our infirmity . . . the Spirit Himself requests for us with groanings unspeakable." For who can describe that which He shows to loving souls in whom He dwells? Who can set forth in words that which He makes them feel? and, lastly, who can explain that for which they long?

2. Assuredly no one can do it; not even they themselves who experience it. That is the reason why they use figures of special comparisons and similitudes; they hide somewhat of that which they feel and in the abundance of the Spirit utter secret mysteries rather than express themselves in clear words.

3. And if these similitudes are not received in the simplicity of a loving mind, and in the sense in which they are uttered, they will seem to be effusions of folly rather than the language of reason; as anyone may see in the divine Canticle of Solomon, and in others of the sacred books, wherein the Holy Spirit, because ordinary and common speech could not convey His meaning, uttered His mysteries in strange terms and similitudes. It follows from this, that after all that the holy doctors have said, and may say, no words of theirs can explain it; nor can words do it; and so, in general, all that is said falls far short of the meaning.

4. The stanzas that follow having been written under influence of that love which proceeds from the overflowing mystical intelligence, cannot be fully explained. Indeed I do not purpose any such thing, for my sole object is to throw some general light over them, which in my opinion is the better course. It is better to leave the outpourings of love in their own fullness, that everyone may apply them according to the measure of his spirit and power, than to pare them down to one particular sense which is not suited to the taste of everyone. And though I do put forth a particular explanation, still others are not to be bound by it. The mystical wisdom -- that is, the love, of which these stanzas speak -- does not require to be distinctly understood in order to produce the effect of love and tenderness in the soul, for it is in this respect like faith, by which we love God without a clear comprehension of Him.

5. I shall therefore be very concise, though now and then unable to avoid some prolixity where the subject requires it, and when the opportunity is offered of discussing and explaining certain points and effects of prayer: many of which being referred to in these stanzas, I must discuss some of them. I shall, however, pass over the more ordinary ones, and treat briefly of the more extraordinary to which they are subject who, by the mercy of God, have advanced beyond the state of beginners. This I do for two reasons: the first is, that much is already written concerning beginners; and the second is, that I am addressing those who have received from our Lord the grace of being led on from the elementary state and are led inwards to the bosom of His divine love.

6. I therefore trust, though I may discuss some points of scholastic theology relating to the interior commerce of the soul with God, that I am not using such language altogether in vain, and that it will be found profitable for pure spirituality. For though some may be altogether ignorant of scholastic theology by which the divine verities are explained, yet they are not ignorant of mystical theology, the science of love, by which those verities are not only learned, but at the same time are relished also.

7. And in order that what I am going to say may be the better received, I submit myself to higher judgments, and unreservedly to that of our holy mother the Church, intending to say nothing in reliance on my own personal experience, or on what I have observed in other spiritual persons, nor on what I have heard them say -- though I intend to profit by all this -- unless I can confirm it with the sanction of

A Spiritual Canticle of the Soul and the Bridegroom Christ

the divine writings, at least on those points which are most difficult of comprehension.

8. The method I propose to follow in the matter is this: first of all, to cite the words of the text and then to give that explanation of them which belongs to the subject before me. I shall now transcribe all the stanzas and place them at the beginning of this treatise. In the next place, I shall take each of them separately, and explain them line by line, each line in its proper place before the explanation.

Footnotes:

8. [This canticle was made by the Saint when he was in the prison of the Mitigation, in Toledo. It came into the hands of the Venerable Anne of Jesus, at whose request he wrote the following commentary on it, and addressed it to her.]
9. Wisdom 8:1
10. Rom. 8:26

St. John of the Cross

SONG OF THE SOUL AND THE BRIDEGROOM

I

THE BRIDE

>Where have You hidden Yourself,
>And abandoned me in my groaning, O my Beloved?
>You have fled like the hart,
>Having wounded me.
>I ran after You, crying; but You were gone.

II

>O shepherds, you who go
>Through the sheepcots up the hill,
>If you shall see Him
>Whom I love the most,
>Tell Him I languish, suffer, and die.

III

>In search of my Love
>I will go over mountains and strands;
>I will gather no flowers,
>I will fear no wild beasts;
>And pass by the mighty and the frontiers.

IV

>O groves and thickets
>Planted by the hand of the Beloved;
>O verdant meads
>Enameled with flowers,
>Tell me, has He passed by you?

V

ANSWER OF THE CREATURES

>A thousand graces diffusing
>He passed through the groves in haste,
>And merely regarding them
>As He passed
>Clothed them with His beauty.

A Spiritual Canticle of the Soul and the Bridegroom Christ

VI

THE BRIDE

> Oh! who can heal me?
> Give me at once Yourself,
> Send me no more
> A messenger
> Who cannot tell me what I wish.

VII

> All they who serve are telling me
> Of Your unnumbered graces;
> And all wound me more and more,
> And something leaves me dying,
> I know not what, of which they are darkly speaking.

VIII

> But how you persevere, O life,
> Not living where you live;
> The arrows bring death
> Which you receive
> From your conceptions of the Beloved.

IX

> Why, after wounding
> This heart, have You not healed it?
> And why, after stealing it,
> Have You thus abandoned it,
> And not carried away the stolen prey?

X

> Quench my troubles,
> For no one else can soothe them;
> And let my eyes behold You,
> For You are their light,
> And I will keep them for You alone.

XI

> Reveal Your presence,
> And let the vision and Your beauty kill me,
> Behold the malady
> Of love is incurable
> Except in Your presence and before Your face.

XII

> O crystal well!
> Oh that on Your silvered surface
> You would mirror forth at once
> Those eyes desired
> Which are outlined in my heart!

St. John of the Cross

XIII

Turn them away, O my Beloved!
I am on the wing:

THE BRIDEGROOM

Return, My Dove!
The wounded hart
Looms on the hill
In the air of your flight and is refreshed.

XIV

My Beloved is the mountains,
The solitary wooded valleys,
The strange islands,
The roaring torrents,
The whisper of the amorous gales;

XV

The tranquil night
At the approaches of the dawn,
The silent music,
The murmuring solitude,
The supper which revives, and enkindles love.

XVI

Catch us the foxes,
For our vineyard has flourished;
While of roses
We make a nosegay,
And let no one appear on the hill.

XVII

O killing north wind, cease!
Come, south wind, that awakens love!
Blow through my garden,
And let its odors flow,
And the Beloved shall feed among the flowers.

XVIII

O nymphs of Judea!
While amid the flowers and the rose-trees
The amber sends forth its perfume,
Tarry in the suburbs,
And touch not our thresholds.

XIX

Hide yourself, O my Beloved!
Turn Your face to the mountains,
Do not speak,
But regard the companions
Of her who is traveling amidst strange islands.

A Spiritual Canticle of the Soul and the Bridegroom Christ

XX

THE BRIDEGROOM

> Light-winged birds,
> Lions, fawns, bounding does,
> Mountains, valleys, strands,
> Waters, winds, heat,
> And the terrors that keep watch by night;

XXI

> By the soft lyres
> And the siren strains, I adjure you,
> Let your fury cease,
> And touch not the wall,
> That the bride may sleep in greater security.

XXII

> The bride has entered
> The pleasant and desirable garden,
> And there reposes to her heart's content;
> Her neck reclining
> On the sweet arms of the Beloved.

XXIII

> Beneath the apple-tree
> There were you betrothed;
> There I gave you My hand,
> And you were redeemed
> Where your mother was corrupted.

XXIV

THE BRIDE

> Our bed is of flowers
> By dens of lions encompassed,
> Hung with purple,
> Made in peace,
> And crowned with a thousand shields of gold.

XXV

> In Your footsteps
> The young ones run Your way;
> At the touch of the fire
> And by the spiced wine,
> The divine balsam flows.

XXVI

> In the inner cellar
> Of my Beloved have I drunk; and when I went forth
> Over all the plain
> I knew nothing,
> And lost the flock I followed before.

XXVII

There He gave me His breasts,
There He taught me the science full of sweetness.
And there I gave to Him
Myself without reserve;
There I promised to be His bride.

XXVIII

My soul is occupied,
And all my substance in His service;
Now I guard no flock,
Nor have I any other employment:
My sole occupation is love.

XXIX

If, then, on the common land
I am no longer seen or found,
You will say that I am lost;
That, being enamored,
I lost myself; and yet was found.

XXX

Of emeralds, and of flowers
In the early morning gathered,
We will make the garlands,
Flowering in Your love,
And bound together with one hair of my head.

XXXI

By that one hair
You have observed fluttering on my neck,
And on my neck regarded,
You were captivated;
And wounded by one of my eyes.

XXXII

When You regarded me,
Your eyes imprinted in me Your grace:
For this You loved me again,
And thereby my eyes merited
To adore what in You they saw

XXXIII

Despise me not,
For if I was swarthy once
You can regard me now;
Since You have regarded me,
Grace and beauty have You given me.

A Spiritual Canticle of the Soul and the Bridegroom Christ

XXXIV

THE BRIDEGROOM

>The little white dove
>Has returned to the ark with the bough;
>And now the turtle-dove
>Its desired mate
>On the green banks has found.

XXXV

>In solitude she lived,
>And in solitude built her nest;
>And in solitude, alone
>Has the Beloved guided her,
>In solitude also wounded with love.

XXXVI

THE BRIDE

>Let us rejoice, O my Beloved!
>Let us go forth to see ourselves in Your beauty,
>To the mountain and the hill,
>Where the pure water flows:
>Let us enter into the heart of the thicket.

XXXVII

>We shall go at once
>To the deep caverns of the rock
>Which are all secret,
>There we shall enter in
>And taste of the new wine of the pomegranate.

XXXVIII

>There you will show me
>That which my soul desired;
>And there You will give at once,
>O You, my life!
>That which You gave me the other day.

XXXIX

>The breathing of the air,
>The song of the sweet nightingale,
>The grove and its beauty
>In the serene night,
>With the flame that consumes, and gives no pains.

XL

>None saw it;
>Neither did Aminadab appear
>The siege was intermitted,
>And the cavalry dismounted
>At the sight of the waters.

ARGUMENT

THESE stanzas describe the career of a soul from its first entrance on the service of God till it comes to the final state of perfection -- the spiritual marriage. They refer accordingly to the three states or ways of the spiritual training -- the purgative, illuminative, and unitive ways, some properties and effects of which they explain.

The first stanzas relate to beginners -- to the purgative way. The second to the advanced -- to the state of spiritual betrothal; that is, the illuminative way. The next to the unitive way -- that of the perfect, the spiritual Marriage. The unitive way, that of the perfect, follows the illuminative, which is that of the advanced.

The last stanzas treat of the beatific state, which only the already perfect soul aims at.

EXPLANATION OF THE STANZAS

NOTE

THE soul, considering the obligations of its state, seeing that "the days of man are short;" [11] that the way of eternal life is straight; [12] that "the just man shall scarcely be saved;" [13] that the things of this world are empty and deceitful; that all die and perish like water poured on the ground; [14] that time is uncertain, the last account strict, perdition most easy, and salvation most difficult; and recognizing also, on the other hand, the great debt that is owing to God, Who has created it solely for Himself, for which the service of its whole life is due, Who has redeemed it for Himself alone, for which it owes Him all else, and the correspondence of its will to His love; and remembering other innumerable blessings for which it acknowledges itself indebted to God even before it was born: and also that a great part of its life has been wasted, and that it will have to render an account of it all from beginning to the end, to the payment of "the last farthing," [15] when God shall "search Jerusalem with lamps;" [16] that it is already late, and perhaps the end of the day: [17] in order to remedy so great an evil, especially when it is conscious that God is grievously offended, and that He has hidden His face from it, because it would forget Him for the creature,-the soul, now touched with sorrow and inward sinking of the heart at the sight of its imminent risks and ruin, renouncing everything and casting them aside without delaying for a day, or even an hour, with fear and groanings uttered from the heart, and wounded with the love of God, begins to invoke the Beloved and says:

Footnotes:

11. Job 14:5
12. Matt. 7:14
13. 1 Pet. 4:18
14. 2 Kings 14:14
15. Matt. 5:26
16. Sophon, 1. 12.
17. Matt. 20:6

A Spiritual Canticle of the Soul and the Bridegroom Christ

STANZA I

THE BRIDE

> *Where have You hidden Yourself,*
> *And abandoned me to my sorrow, O my Beloved!*
> *You have fled like the hart,*
> *Having wounded me.*
> *I ran after You, crying; but You were gone.*

IN this first stanza the soul, enamored of the Word, the Son of God, the Bridegroom, desiring to be united to Him in the clear and substantial vision, sets before Him the anxieties of its love, complaining of His absence. And this the more so because, now pierced and wounded with love, for which it had abandoned all things, even itself, it has still to endure the absence of the Beloved, Who has not released it from its mortal flesh, that it might have the fruition of Him in the glory of eternity. Hence it cries out,

"*Where have You hidden Yourself?*"

2. It is as if the soul said, "Show me, O You the Word, my Bridegroom, the place where You are hidden." It asks for the revelation of the divine Essence; for the place where the Son of God is hidden is, according to St. John, "the bosom of the Father,"[18] which is the divine Essence, transcending all mortal vision, and hidden from all human understanding, as Isaiah says, speaking to God, "Verily You are a hidden God."[19] From this we learn that the communication and sense of His presence, however great they may be, and the most sublime and profound knowledge of God which the soul may have in this life, are not God essentially, neither have they any affinity with Him, for in very truth He is still hidden from the soul; and it is therefore expedient for it, amid all these grandeurs, always to consider Him as hidden, and to seek Him in His hiding place, saying,

"*Where have You hidden Yourself?*"

3. Neither sublime communications nor sensible presence furnish any certain proof of His gracious presence; nor is the absence thereof, and aridity, any proof of His absence from the soul. "If He come to me, I shall not see Him; if He depart, I shall not understand."[20] That is, if the soul have any great communication, or impression, or spiritual knowledge, it must not on that account persuade itself that what it then feels is to enjoy or see God clearly and in His Essence, or that it brings it nearer to Him, or Him to it, however deep such feelings may be. On the other hand, when all these sensible and spiritual communications fail it, and it is itself in dryness, darkness, and desolation, it must not on that account suppose that God is far from it; for in truth the former state is no sign of its being in a state of grace, nor is the latter a sign that it is not; for "man knows not whether he is worthy of love or hatred"[21] in the sight of God.

4. The chief object of the soul in these words is not to ask only for that affective and sensible devotion, wherein there is no certainty or evidence of the possession of the Bridegroom in this life; but principally for that clear presence and vision of His Essence, of which it longs to be assured and satisfied in the next. This, too, was the object of the bride who, in the divine song desiring to be united to the Divinity of the Bridegroom Word, prayed to the Father, saying, "Show me where You feed, where You lie in the midday."[22] For to ask to be shown the place where He fed was to ask to be shown the Essence of the Divine Word, the Son; because the Father feeds nowhere else but in His only begotten Son, Who is the glory of the Father. In asking to be shown the place where He lies in the midday, was to ask for the same thing, because the Son is the sole delight of the Father, Who lies in no other place, and is comprehended by no other thing, but in and by His beloved Son, in Whom He reposes wholly, communicating to Him His whole Essence, in the "midday," which is eternity, where the Father is ever begetting and the Son ever begotten.

5. This pasture, then, is the Bridegroom Word, where the Father feeds in infinite glory. He is also

the bed of flowers whereupon He reposes with infinite delight of love, profoundly hidden from all mortal vision and every created thing. This is the meaning of the bride-soul when she says,

"Where have You hidden Yourself?"

6. That the thirsty soul may find the Bridegroom, and be one with Him in the union of love in this life -- so far as that is possible -- and quench its thirst with that drink which it is possible to drink of at His hands in this life, it will be as well -- since that is what the Soul asks of Him -- that we should answer for Him, and point out the special spot where He is hidden, that He may be found there in that perfection and sweetness of which this life is capable, and that the soul may not begin to loiter uselessly in the footsteps of its companions.

7. We must remember that the Word, the Son of God, together with the Father and the Holy Spirit, is hidden in essence and in presence, in the inmost being of the soul. That soul, therefore, that will find Him, must go out from all things in will and affection, and enter into the profoundest self-recollection, and all things must be to it as if they existed not. Hence, St. Augustine says: "I found You not without, O Lord; I sought You without in vain, for You are within,"[23] God is therefore hidden within the soul, and the true contemplative will seek Him there in love, saying,

"Where have You hidden Yourself?"

8. O you soul, then, most beautiful of creatures, who so long to know the place where your Beloved is, that you may seek Him, and be united to Him, you know now that you are yourself that very tabernacle where He dwells, the secret chamber of His retreat where He is hidden. Rejoice, therefore, and exult, because all your good and all your hope is so near you as to be within you; or, to speak more accurately, that you can not be without it, "for lo, the kingdom of God is within you."[24] So says the Bridegroom Himself, and His servant, St. Paul, adds: "You are the temple of the living God."[25] What joy for the soul to learn that God never abandons it, even in mortal sin; how much less in a state of grace![26]

9. What more can you desire, what more can you seek without, seeing that within you have your riches, your delight, your satisfaction, your fullness and your kingdom; that is, your Beloved, Whom you desire and seek? Rejoice, then, and be glad in Him with interior recollection, seeing that you have Him so near. Then love Him, then desire Him, then adore Him, and go not to seek Him out of yourself, for that will be but distraction and weariness, and you shall not find Him; because there is no fruition of Him more certain, more ready, or more intimate than that which is within.

10. One difficulty alone remains: though He is within, yet He is hidden. But it is a great matter to know the place of His secret rest, that He may be sought there with certainty. The knowledge of this is that which you ask for here, O soul, when with loving affection you cry,

"Where have You hidden Yourself?"

11. You will still urge and say, How is it, then, that I find Him not, nor feel Him, if He is within my soul? It is because He is hidden, and because you hide not yourself also that you may find Him and feel Him; for he that will seek that which is hidden must enter secretly into the secret place where it is hidden, and when he finds it, he is himself hidden like the object of his search. Seeing, then, that the Bridegroom whom you love is "the treasure hidden in the field"[27] of your soul, for which the wise merchant gave all that he had, so you, if you will find Him, must forget all that is yours, withdraw from all created things, and hide yourself in the secret retreat of the spirit, shutting the door upon yourself -- that is, denying your will in all things -- and praying to your Father in secret.[28] Then you, being hidden with Him, will be conscious of His presence in secret, and will love Him, possess Him in secret, and delight in Him in secret, in a way that no tongue or language can express.

12. Courage, then, O soul most beautiful, you know now that your Beloved, Whom you desire, dwells hidden within your breast; strive, therefore, to be truly hidden with Him, and then you shall embrace Him, and be conscious of His presence with loving affection. Consider also that He bids you, by the mouth of Isaiah, to come to His secret hiding-place, saying, "Go, . . . enter into your chambers, shut your doors upon you"; that is, all your faculties, so that no created thing shall enter: "be hid a little for a moment,"[29] that is, for the moment of this mortal life; for if now during this life which is short, you will "with all watchfulness keep your heart,"[30] as the wise man says, God will most assuredly give you, as He has promised by the prophet Isaiah, "hidden treasures and mysteries of secrets."[31] The substance of these secrets is God Himself, for He is the substance of the faith, and the object of it, and the faith is the secret and the mystery. And when that which the faith conceals shall be revealed and made manifest, that is the perfection of God, as St. Paul says, "When that which is perfect is come,"[32] then shall be revealed to the soul the substance and mysteries of these secrets.

A Spiritual Canticle of the Soul and the Bridegroom Christ

13. Though in this mortal life the soul will never reach to the interior secrets as it will in the next, however much it may hide itself, still, if it will hide itself with Moses, "in the hole of the rock" -- which is a real imitation of the perfect life of the Bridegroom, the Son of God -- protected by the right hand of God, it will merit the vision of the "back parts"; [33] that is, it will reach to such perfection here, as to be united, and transformed by love, in the Son of God, its Bridegroom. So effectually will this be wrought that the soul will feel itself so united to Him, so learned and so instructed in His secrets, that, so far as the knowledge of Him in this life is concerned, it will be no longer necessary for it to say: "Where have You hidden Yourself?"

14. You know then, O soul, how you are to demean yourself if you will find the Bridegroom in His secret place. But if you will hear it again, hear this one word full of substance and unapproachable truth: Seek Him in faith and love, without seeking to satisfy yourself in anything, or to understand more than is expedient for you to know; for faith and love are the two guides of the blind; they will lead you, by a way you know not, to the secret chamber of God. Faith, the secret of which I am speaking, is the foot that journeys onwards to God, and love is the guide that directs its steps. And while the soul meditates on the mysterious secrets of the faith, it will merit the revelation, on the part of love, of that which the faith involves, namely, the Bridegroom Whom it longs for, in this life by spiritual grace, and the divine union, as we said before, [34] and in the next in essential glory, face to face, hidden now.

15. But meanwhile, though the soul attains to union, the highest state possible in this life, yet inasmuch as He is still hidden from it in the bosom of the Father, as I have said, the soul longing for the fruition of Him in the life to come, ever cries, "Where have You hidden Yourself?"

16. You do well, then, O soul, in seeking Him always in His secret place; for you greatly magnify God, and draw near to Him, esteeming Him as far beyond and above all you can reach. Rest, therefore, neither wholly nor in part, on what your faculties can embrace; never seek to satisfy yourself with what you comprehend of God, but rather with what you comprehend not; and never rest on the love of, and delight in, that which you can understand and feel, but rather on that which is beyond your understanding and feeling: this is, as I have said, to seek Him by faith.

17. God is, as I said before, [35] inaccessible and hidden, and though it may seem that you have found Him, felt Him, and comprehended Him, yet you must ever regard Him as hidden, serve Him as hidden, in secret. Do not be like many unwise, who, with low views of God, think that when they cannot comprehend Him, or be conscious of His presence, that He is then farther away and more hidden, when the contrary is true, namely, that He is nearer to them when they are least aware of it; as the prophet David says, "He put darkness His covert," [36] Thus, when you are near to Him, the very infirmity of your vision makes the darkness palpable; you do well, therefore, at all times, in prosperity as well as in adversity, spiritual or temporal, to look upon God as hidden, and to say to Him, "Where have You hidden Yourself?"

And left me to my sorrow, O my Beloved?"

18. The soul calls Him "my Beloved," the more to move Him to listen to its cry, for God, when loved, most readily listens to the prayer of him who loves Him. Thus He speaks Himself: "If you abide in Me . . . you shall ask whatever thing you will, and it shall be done to you." [37] The soul may then with truth call Him Beloved, when it is wholly His, when the heart has no attachments but Him, and when all the thoughts are continually directed to Him. It was the absence of this that made Delilah say to Samson, "How do you say you love me when your mind is not with me?" [38] The mind comprises the thoughts and the feelings. Some there are who call the Bridegroom their Beloved, but He is not really beloved, because their heart is not wholly with Him. Their prayers are, therefore, not so effectual before God, and they shall not obtain their petitions until, persevering in prayer, they fix their minds more constantly upon God and their hearts more wholly in loving affection upon Him, for nothing can be obtained from God but by love.

19. The words, "And left me to my sorrow," tell us that the absence of the Beloved is the cause of continual sadness in him who loves; for as such a one loves none else, so, in the absence of the object beloved, nothing can console or relieve him. This is, therefore, a test to discern the true lover of God. Is he satisfied with anything less than God? Do I say satisfied? Yes, if a man possess all things, he cannot be satisfied; the greater his possessions the less will be his satisfaction, for the satisfaction of the heart is not found in possessions, but in detachment from all things and in poverty of spirit. This being so, the perfection of love in which we possess God, by a grace most intimate and special, lives in the soul in this life when it has reached it, with a certain satisfaction, which however is not full, for David, notwithstanding all his perfection, hoped for that in heaven saying, "I shall be satisfied when Your glory shall appear." [39]

20. Thus, then, the peace and tranquillity and satisfaction of heart to which the soul may attain in this life are not sufficient to relieve it from its groaning, peaceful and painless though it be, while it hopes for that which is still wanting. Groaning belongs to hope, as the Apostle says of himself and

others, though perfect, "Ourselves also, who have the first fruits of the Spirit, even we ourselves groan within ourselves, waiting for the adoption of the sons of God." [40] The soul groans when the heart is enamored, for where love wounds there is heard the groaning of the wounded one, complaining feelingly of the absence of the Beloved, especially when, after tasting of the sweet conversation of the Bridegroom, it finds itself suddenly alone, and in aridity, because He has gone away. That is why it cries,

"You have fled like the hart."

21. Here it is to be observed that in the Canticle of Canticles the bride compares the Bridegroom to the roe and the hart on the mountains -- "My Beloved is like a roe and to a fawn of harts" [41] -- not only because He is shy, solitary, and avoids companions as the hart, but also for his sudden appearance and disappearance. That is His way in His visits to devout souls in order to comfort and encourage them, and in the withdrawing and absence which He makes them feel after those visits in order to try, humble, and teach them. For that purpose He makes them feel the pain of His absence most keenly, as the following words show:

"Having wounded me."

22. It is as if it had said, "It was not enough that I should feel the pain and grief which Your absence causes, and from which I am continually suffering, but You must, after wounding me with the arrow of Your love, and increasing my longing and desire to see You, run away from me with the swiftness of the hart, and not permit me to lay hold of You, even for a moment."

23. For the clearer understanding of this we are to keep in mind that, beside the many kinds of God's visits to the soul, in which He wounds it with love, there are commonly certain secret touches of love, which, like a fiery arrow, pierce and penetrate the soul, and burn it with the fire of love. These are properly called the wounds of love, and it is of these the soul is here speaking. These wounds so inflame the will, that the soul becomes so enveloped with the fire of love as to appear consumed thereby. They make it go forth out of itself, and be renewed, and enter on another life, as the phoenix from the fire.

24. David, speaking of this, says, "My heart has been inflamed, and my reins have been changed; and I am brought to nothing, and I knew not." [42] The desires and affections, called the reins by the prophet, are all stirred and divinely changed in this burning of the heart, and the soul, through love, melted into nothing, knowing nothing but love. At this time the changing of the reins is a great pain, and longing for the vision of God; it seems to the soul that God treats it with intolerable severity, so much so that the severity with which love treats it seems to the soul unendurable, not because it is wounded --for it considers such wounds to be its salvation -- but because it is thus suffering from its love, and because He has not wounded it more deeply so as to cause death, that it may be united to Him in the life of perfect love. The soul, therefore, magnifying its sorrows, or revealing them, says,

"Having wounded me."

25. The soul says in effect, "You have abandoned me after wounding me, and You have left me dying of love; and then You have hidden Yourself as a hart swiftly running away." This impression is most profound in the soul; for by the wound of love, made in the soul by God, the affections of the will lead most rapidly to the possession of the Beloved, whose touch it felt, and as rapidly also, His absence, and its inability to have the fruition of Him here as it desires. Thereupon succeed the groaning because of His absence; for these visitations of God are not like those which recreate and satisfy the soul, because they are rather for wounding than for healing -- more for afflicting than for satisfying it, seeing that they tend rather to quicken the knowledge, and increase the longing, and consequently pain with the longing for the vision of God. They are called the spiritual wounds of love, most sweet to the soul and desirable; and, therefore, when it is thus wounded the soul would willingly die a thousand deaths, because these wounds make it go forth out of itself, and enter into God, which is the meaning of the words that follow:

"I ran after You, crying; but You were gone."

26. There can be no remedy for the wounds of love but from Him who inflicted them. And so the wounded soul, urged by the vehemence of that burning which the wounds of love occasion, runs after the Beloved, crying to Him for relief. This spiritual running after God has a two-fold meaning. The first is a going forth from all created things, which is effected by hating and despising them; the second, a going forth out of oneself, by forgetting self, which is brought about by the love of God. For when the love of God touches the soul with that vividness of which we are here speaking, it so elevates it, that it

A Spiritual Canticle of the Soul and the Bridegroom Christ

goes forth not only out of itself by self-forgetfulness, but it is also drawn away from its own judgment, natural ways and inclinations, crying after God, "O my Bridegroom," as if saying, "By this touch of Yours and wound of love have You drawn me away not only from all created things, but also from myself -- for, in truth, soul and body seem now to part -- and raised me up to Yourself, crying after You in detachment from all things that I might be attached to You:

"You were gone."

27. As if saying, "When I sought Your presence, I found You not; and I was detached from all things without being able to cling to You --borne painfully by the gales of love without help in You or in myself." This going forth of the soul in search of the Beloved is the rising of the bride in the Canticle: "I will rise and go about the city; in the streets and the high ways I will seek Him Whom my soul loves. I have sought Him and have not found . . . they wounded me." [43] The rising of the bride -- speaking spiritually -- is from that which is mean to that which is noble; and is the same with the going forth of the soul out of its own ways and inferior love to the ennobling love of God. The bride says that she was wounded because she found him not; [44] so the soul also says of itself that it is wounded with love and forsaken; that is, the loving soul is ever in pain during the absence of the Beloved, because it has given itself up wholly to Him hoping for the reward of its self-surrender, the Possession of the Beloved. Still the Beloved withholds Himself while the soul has lost all things, and even itself, for Him; it obtains no compensation for its loss, seeing that it is deprived of Him whom it loves.

28. This pain and sense of the absence of God is wont to be so oppressive in those who are going onwards to the state of perfection, that they would die if God did not interpose when the divine wounds are inflicted upon them. As they have the palate of the will wholesome, and the mind pure and disposed for God, and as they taste in some degree of the sweetness of divine love, which they supremely desire, so they also suffer supremely; for, having but a glimpse of an infinite good which they are not permitted to enjoy, that is to them an ineffable pain and torment.

Footnotes:

18. John 1:18
19. Isa. 45:15
20. Job 9:11
21. Eccles. 9:1
22. Cant. 1:6
23. Soliloq.,' c. 31. Opp. Ed. Ben. tom. vi. app. p. 98.
24. Luke 17:21
25. 2 Cor. 6:16
26. Mt. Carmel,' Bk. 2, c. 5. sect. 3.
27. Matt. 13:44
28. Matt. 6:6
29. Isa. 26:20
30. Prov. 4:23
31. Isa. 45:3
32. 1 Cor. 13:10
33. Exod. 33:22, 23
34. Sect. 4.
35. Sect. 2.
36. Ps. 17:12
37. John 15:7
38. Judg. 16:15
39. Ps. 16:15
40. Rom. 8:23
41. Cant. 2:9
42. Ps. 72:21, 22
43. Cant. 3:2, 5:7
44. Cant. 5:6, 7

STANZA II

O shepherds, you who go
Through the sheepcots up the hill,
If you shall see
Him Whom I love,
Tell Him I languish, suffer, and die.

THE soul would now employ intercessors and mediators between itself and the Beloved, praying them to make its sufferings and afflictions known. One in love, when he cannot converse personally with the object of his love, will do so in the best way he can. Thus the soul employs its affections, desires, and groanings as messengers well able to manifest the secret of its heart to the Beloved. Accordingly, it calls upon them to do this, saying:

"O shepherds, you who go."

2. The shepherds are the affections, and desires, and groanings of the soul, for they feed it with spiritual good things. A shepherd is one who feeds: and by means of such God communicates Himself to the soul and feeds it in the divine pastures; for without these groans and desires He communicates but slightly with it.

"You who go."

You who go forth in pure love; for all desires and affections do not reach God, but only those which proceed from sincere love.

"Through the sheepcots up the hill."

3. The sheepcots are the heavenly hierarchies, the angelic choirs, by whose ministry, from choir to choir, our prayers and sighs ascend to God; that is, to the hill, "for He is the highest eminence, and because in Him, as on a hill, we observe and behold all things, the higher and the lower sheepcots." To Him our prayers ascend, offered by angels, as I have said; so the angel said to Tobit "When you prayed with tears, and buried the dead . . . I offered your prayer to the Lord." [45]

4. The shepherds also are the angels themselves, who not only carry our petitions to God, but also bring down the graces of God to our souls, feeding them like good shepherds, with the sweet communications and inspirations of God, Who employs them in that ministry. They also protect us and defend us against the wolves, which are the evil spirits. And thus, whether we understand the affections or the angels by the shepherds, the soul calls upon both to be its messengers to the Beloved, and thus addresses them all:

"If you shall see Him,"

That is to say:

5. If, to my great happiness you shall come into His presence, so that He shall see you and hear your words. God, indeed, knows all things, even the very thoughts of the soul, as He said to Moses,[46] but it is then He beholds our necessities when He relieves them, and hears our prayers when he grants them. God does not see all necessities and hear all petitions until the time appointed shall have come; it is then that He is said to hear and see, as we learn in the book of Exodus. When the children of Israel had been afflicted for four hundred years as serfs in Egypt, God said to Moses, "I have seen the affliction of my people in Egypt, and I have heard their cry, and . . . I am come down to deliver them."[47] And yet He had seen it always. So also St. Gabriel bade Zachariah not to fear, because God had heard his prayer, and would grant him the son, for whom he had been praying for many years;[48] yet God had always heard him. Every soul ought to consider that God, though He does not at once help us and grant

A Spiritual Canticle of the Soul and the Bridegroom Christ

our petitions, will still succor us in His own time, for He is, as David says, "a helper in due time in tribulation," [49] if we do not become faint-hearted and cease to pray. This is what the soul means by saying, "If you shall see Him"; that is to say, if the time is come when it shall be His good pleasure to grant my petitions.

6. "Whom I love the most": that is, whom I love more than all creatures. This is true of the soul when nothing can make it afraid to do and suffer all things in His service. And when the soul can also truly say that which follows, it is a sign that it loves Him above all things:

"Tell Him I languish, suffer, and die."

7. Here the soul speaks of three things that distress it: namely, languor, suffering, and death; for the soul that truly loves God with a love in some degree perfect, suffers in three ways in His absence, in its three powers ordinarily -- the understanding, the will, and the memory. In the understanding it languishes because it does not see God, Who is the salvation of it, as the Psalmist says: "I am your salvation." [50] In the will it suffers, because it possesses not God, Who is its comfort and delight, as David also says: "You shall make them drink of the torrent of Your pleasure." [51] In the memory it dies, because it remembers its privation of all the blessings of the understanding, which are the vision of God, and of the delights of the will, which are the fruition of Him, and that it is very possible also that it may lose Him for ever, because of the dangers and chances of this life. In the memory, therefore, the soul labors under a sensation like that of death, because it sees itself without the certain and perfect fruition of God, Who is the life of the soul, as Moses says: "He is your life." [52]

8. Jeremiah also, in the Lamentations, speaks of these three things, praying to God, and saying: "Remember my poverty . . . the wormwood and the gall." [53] Poverty relates to the understanding, to which appertain the riches of the knowledge of the Son of God, "in whom all the treasures of wisdom and knowledge are hid." [54] The wormwood, which is a most bitter herb, relates to the will, to which appertains the sweetness of the fruition of God, deprived of which it abides in bitterness. We learn in the Revelation that bitterness appertains spiritually to the will, for the angel said to St. John: "Take the book and eat it up; and it shall make your belly bitter." [55] Here the belly signifies the will. The gall relates not only to the memory, but also to all the powers and faculties of the soul, for it signifies the death thereof, as we learn from Moses speaking of the damned: "Their wine is the gall of dragons, and the venom of asps, which is incurable." [56] This signifies the loss of God, which is the death of the soul.

9. These three things which distress the soul are grounded on the three theological virtues -- faith, charity, and hope, which relate, in the order here assigned them, to the three faculties of the soul -- understanding, will, and memory. Observe here that the soul does no more than represent its miseries and pain to the Beloved: for he who loves wisely does not care to ask for that which he wants and desires, being satisfied with hinting at his necessities, so that the beloved one may do what shall to him seem good. Thus the Blessed Virgin at the marriage feast of Cana asked not directly for wine, but only said to her Beloved Son, "They have no wine." [57] The sisters of Lazarus sent to Him, not to ask Him to heal their brother, but only to say that he whom He loved was sick: "Lord, behold, he whom You love is sick." [58]

10. There are three reasons for this. Our Lord knows what is expedient for us better than we do ourselves. Secondly, the Beloved is more compassionate towards us when He sees our necessities and our resignation. Thirdly, we are more secured against self-love and self-seeking when we represent our necessity, than when we ask for that which we think we need. It is in this way that the soul represents its three necessities; as if it said: "Tell my Beloved, that as I languish, and as He only is my salvation, to save me; that as I am suffering, and as He only is my joy, to give me joy; that as I am dying, and as He only is my life, to give me life."

Footnotes:

45. Tob. 12:12
46. Deut. 31:21
47. Exod. 3:7, 8
48. Luke 1:13
49. Ps. 9:10
50. Ps. 34:3
51. Ps. 35:9
52. Deut. 30:20
53. Lam. 3:19
54. Col. 2:3
55. Rev. 10:9
56. Deut. 32:33

57. John 2:3
58. John 11:3

A Spiritual Canticle of the Soul and the Bridegroom Christ

STANZA III

*In search of my Love
I will go over mountains and strands;
I will gather no flowers,
I will fear no wild beasts;
And pass by the mighty and the frontiers.*

THE soul, observing that its sighs and prayers suffice not to find the Beloved, and that it has not been helped by the messengers it invoked in the first and second stanzas, will not, because its searching is real and its love great, leave undone anything itself can do. The soul that really loves God is not dilatory in its efforts to find the Son of God, its Beloved; and, even when it has done all it could it is still not satisfied, thinking it has done nothing. Accordingly, the soul is now, in this third stanza, actively seeking the Beloved, and saying how He is to be found; namely, in the practice of all virtue and in the spiritual exercises of the active and contemplative life; for this end it rejects all delights and all comforts; and all the power and wiles of its three enemies, the world, the devil, and the flesh, are unable to delay it or hinder it on the road.

"In search of my Love."

2. Here the soul makes it known that to find God it is not enough to pray with the heart and the tongue, or to have recourse to the help of others; we must also work ourselves, according to our power. God values one effort of our own more than many of others on our behalf; the soul, therefore, remembering the saying of the Beloved, "Seek and you shall find," [59] is resolved on going forth, as I said just now, to seek Him actively, and not rest till it finds Him, as many do who will not that God should cost them anything but words, and even those carelessly uttered, and for His sake will do nothing that will cost them anything. Some, too, will not leave for His sake a place which is to their taste and liking, expecting to receive all the sweetness of God in their mouth and in their heart without moving a step, without mortifying themselves by the abandonment of a single pleasure or useless comfort.

3. But until they go forth out of themselves to seek Him, however loudly they may cry they will not find Him; for the bride in the Canticle sought Him in this way, but she found Him not until she went out to seek Him: "In my little bed in the nights I have sought Him Whom my soul loves: I have sought Him and have not found Him. I will rise and will go about the city: by the streets and highways I will seek Him Whom my soul loves." [60] She afterwards adds that when she had endured certain trials she "found Him." [61]

4. He, therefore, who seeks God, consulting his own ease and comfort, seeks Him by night, and therefore finds Him not. But he who seeks Him in the practice of virtue and of good works, casting aside the comforts of his own bed, seeks Him by day; such a one shall find Him, for that which is not seen by night is visible by day. The Bridegroom Himself teaches us this, saying, "Wisdom is clear and never fades away, and is easily seen of them that love her, and is found of them that seek her. She prevents them that covet her, that she first may show herself to them. He that awakes early to seek her shall not labor; for he shall find her sitting at his doors." [62] The soul that will go out of the house of its own will, and abandon the bed of its own satisfaction, will find the divine Wisdom, the Son of God, the Bridegroom waiting at the door without, and so the soul says:

"I will go over mountains and strands."

5. Mountains, which are lofty, signify virtues, partly on account of their height and partly on account of the toil and labor of ascending them; the soul says it will ascend to them in the practice of the contemplative life. Strands, which are low, signify mortifications, penances, and the spiritual exercises, and the soul will add to the active life that of contemplation; for both are necessary in seeking after God and in acquiring virtue. The soul says, in effect, "In searching after my Beloved I will practice great virtue, and abase myself by lowly mortifications and acts of humility, for the way to seek God is to do good works in Him, and to mortify the evil in ourselves, as it is said in the words that follow:

"I will gather no flowers."

6. He that will seek after God must have his heart detached, resolute, and free from all evils, and from all goods which are not simply God; that is the meaning of these words. The words that follow describe the liberty and courage which the soul must possess in searching after God. Here it declares that it will gather no flowers by the way -- the flowers are all the delights, satisfactions, and pleasures which this life offers, and which, if the soul sought or accepted, would hinder it on the road.

7. These flowers are of three kinds -- temporal, sensual, and spiritual. All of them occupy the heart, and stand in the way of the spiritual detachment required in the way of Christ, if we regard them or rest in them. The soul, therefore, says, that it will not stop to gather any of them, that it may seek after God. It seems to say, I will not set my heart upon riches or the goods of this world; I will not indulge in the satisfactions and ease of the flesh, neither will I consult the taste and comforts of my spirit, in order that nothing may detain me in my search after my Love on the toilsome mountains of virtue. This means that it accepts the counsel of the prophet David to those who travel on this road: "If riches abound, set not your heart upon them," [63] This is applicable to sensual satisfactions, as well as to temporal goods and spiritual consolations.

8. From this we learn that not only temporal goods and bodily pleasures hinder us on the road to God, but spiritual delight and consolations also, if we attach ourselves to them or seek them; for these things are hindrances on the way of the cross of Christ, the Bridegroom. He, therefore, that will go onwards must not only not stop to gather flowers, but must also have the courage and resolution to say as follows:

"I will fear no wild beasts and I will go over the mighty and the frontiers."

Here we have the three enemies of the soul which make war against it, and make its way full of difficulties. The wild beasts are the world; the mighty, the devil; and the frontiers are the flesh.

9. The world is the wild beasts, because in the beginning of the heavenly journey the imagination pictures the world to the soul as wild beasts, threatening and fierce, principally in three ways. The first is, we must forfeit the world's favor, lose friends, credit, reputation, and property; the second is not less cruel: we must suffer the perpetual deprivation of all the comforts and pleasures of the world; and the third is still worse: evil tongues will rise against us, mock us, and speak of us with contempt. This strikes some persons so vividly that it becomes most difficult for them, I do not say to persevere, but even to enter on this road at all.

10. But there are generous souls who have to encounter wild beasts of a more interior and spiritual nature -- trials, temptations, tribulations, and afflictions of diverse kinds, through which they must pass. This is what God sends to those whom He is raising upwards to high perfection, proving them and trying them as gold in the fire; as David says: "Many are the tribulations of the just; and out of all these our Lord will deliver them." [64] But the truly enamored soul, preferring the Beloved above all things, and relying on His love and favor, finds no difficulty in saying:

"I will fear no wild beats" "and pass over the mighty and the frontiers."

11. Evil spirits, the second enemy of the soul, are called the mighty, because they strive with all their might to seize on the passes of the spiritual road; and because the temptations they suggest are harder to overcome, and the craft they employ more difficult to detect, than all the seductions of the world and the flesh; and because, also, they strengthen their own position by the help of the world and the flesh in order to fight vigorously against the soul. Hence the Psalmist calls them mighty, saying: "The mighty have sought after my soul." [65] The prophet Job also speaks of their might: "There is no power upon the earth that may be compared with him who was made to fear no man." [66]

12. There is no human power that can be compared with the power of the devil, and therefore the divine power alone can overcome him, and the divine light alone can penetrate his devices. No soul therefore can overcome his might without prayer, or detect his illusions without humility and mortification. Hence the exhortation of St. Paul to the faithful: "Put on the armor of God, that you may stand against the deceits of the devil: for our wrestling is not against flesh and blood." [67] Blood here is the world, and the armor of God is prayer and the cross of Christ, wherein consist the humility and mortification of which I have spoken.

13. The soul says also that it will cross the frontiers: these are the natural resistance and rebellion of the flesh against the spirit, for, as St. Paul says, the "flesh lusts against the spirit," [68] and sets itself as a frontier against the soul on its spiritual road. This frontier the soul must cross, surmounting difficulties, and trampling underfoot all sensual appetites and all natural affections with great courage and resolution of spirit: for while they remain in the soul, the spirit will be by them hindered from advancing to the true life and spiritual delight. This is set clearly before us by St. Paul, saying: "If by the

A Spiritual Canticle of the Soul and the Bridegroom Christ

spirit you mortify the deeds of the flesh, you shall live."[69] This, then, is the process which the soul in this stanza says it becomes it to observe on the way to seek the Beloved: which briefly is a firm resolution not to stoop to gather flowers by the way; courage not to fear the wild beasts, and strength to pass by the mighty and the frontiers; intent solely on going over the mountains and the strands of the virtues, in the way just explained.

Footnotes:

59. Luke 11:9
60. Cant. 3:1
61. Cant. 3:4
62. Wisd. 6:13
63. Ps. 61:11
64. Ps. 33:20
65. Ps. 53:5
66. Job 41:24
67. Eph. 6:11
68. Gal. 5:17
69. Rom. 8:13

St. John of the Cross

STANZA IV

O groves and thickets
Planted by the hand of the Beloved;
O verdant meads
Enameled with flowers,
Tell me, has He passed by you?

THE disposition requisite for entering on the spiritual journey, abstinence from joys and pleasure, being now described; and the courage also with which to overcome temptations and trials, wherein consists the practice of self-knowledge, which is the first step of the soul to the knowledge of God. Now, in this stanza the soul begins to advance through consideration and knowledge of creatures to the knowledge of the Beloved their Creator. For the consideration of the creature, after the practice of self-knowledge, is the first in order on the spiritual road to the knowledge of God, Whose grandeur and magnificence they declare, as the Apostle says: "For His invisible things from the creation of the world are seen, being understood by these things that are made." [70] It is as if he said, "The invisible things of God are made known to the soul by created things, visible and invisible."

2. The soul, then, in this stanza addresses itself to creatures inquiring after the Beloved. And we observe, as St. Augustine [71] says, that the inquiry made of creatures is a meditation on the Creator, for which they furnish the matter. Thus, in this stanza the soul meditates on the elements and the rest of the lower creation; on the heavens, and on the rest of created and material things which God has made therein; also on the heavenly Spirits, saying:

"O groves and thickets."

3. The groves are the elements, earth, water, air, and fire. As the most pleasant groves are studded with plants and shrubs, so the elements are thick with creatures, and here are called thickets because of the number and variety of creatures in each. The earth contains innumerable varieties of animals and plants, the water of fish, the air of birds, and fire concurs with all in animating and sustaining them. Each kind of animal lives in its proper element, placed and planted there, as in its own grove and soil where it is born and nourished; and, in truth, God so ordered it when He made them; He commanded the earth to bring forth herbs and animals; the waters and the sea, fish; and the air He gave as a habitation to birds. The soul, therefore, considering that this is the effect of His commandment, cries out,

"Planted by the hand of the Beloved."

4. That which the soul considers now is this: the hand of God the Beloved only could have created and nurtured all these varieties and wonderful things. The soul says deliberately, "by the hand of the Beloved," because God does many things by the hands of others, as of angels and men; but the work of creation has never been, and never is, the work of any other hand than His own. Thus the soul, considering the creation, is profoundly stirred up to love God the Beloved for it beholds all things to be the work of His hands, and goes on to say:

"O verdant meads."

5. These are the heavens; for the things which He has created in the heavens are of incorruptible freshness, which neither perish nor wither with time, where the just are refreshed as in the green pastures. The present consideration includes all the varieties of the stars in their beauty, and the other works in the heavens.

6. The Church also applies the term "verdure" to heavenly things; for while praying to God for the departing soul, it addresses it as follows: "May Christ, the Son of the living God, give you a place in the ever-pleasant verdure of His paradise." [72] The soul also says that this verdant mead is

A Spiritual Canticle of the Soul and the Bridegroom Christ
"*Enameled with flowers.*"

7. The flowers are the angels and the holy souls who adorn and beautify that place, as costly and fine enamel on a vase of pure gold.

"*Tell me, has He passed by you?*"

8. This inquiry is the consideration of the creature just spoken of, and is in effect: Tell me, what perfections has He created in you?

Footnotes:

70. Rom. 1:20
71. Conf. 10. 6.
72. Ordo commendationis animae.

St. John of the Cross

STANZA V

ANSWER OF THE CREATURES

A thousand graces diffusing
He passed through the groves in haste,
And merely regarding them
As He passed,
Clothed them with His beauty.

THIS is the answer of the creatures to the soul which, according to St. Augustine, in the same place, is the testimony which they furnish to the majesty and perfections of God, for which it asked in its meditation on created things. The meaning of this stanza is, in substance, as follows: God created all things with great ease and rapidity, and left in them some tokens of Himself, not only by creating them out of nothing, but also by endowing them with innumerable graces and qualities, making them beautiful in admirable order and unceasing mutual dependence. All this He wrought in wisdom, by which He created them, which is the Word, His only begotten Son. Then the soul says;

"*A thousand graces diffusing.*"

2. These graces are the innumerable multitude of His creatures. The term "thousand," which the soul makes use of, denotes not their number, but the impossibility of numbering them. They are called grace because of the qualities with which He has endowed them. He is said to diffuse them because He fills the whole world with them.

"*He passed through the groves in haste.*"

3. To pass through the groves is to create the elements; here called groves, through which He is said to pass, diffusing a thousand graces, because He adorned them with creatures which are all beautiful. Moreover, He diffused among them a thousand graces, giving the power of generation and self-conservation. He is said to pass through, because the creatures are, as it were, traces of the passage of God, revealing His majesty, power, and wisdom, and His other divine attributes. He is said to pass in haste, because the creatures are the least of the works of God: He made them, as it were, in passing. His greatest works, wherein He is most visible and at rest, are the incarnation of the Word and the mysteries of the Christian faith, in comparison with which all His other works were works wrought in passing and in haste.

"*And thereby regarding them As He passed, Clothed them with His beauty.*"

4. The son of God is, in the words of St. Paul, "the brightness of His glory and the figure of His substance." [73] God saw all things only in the face of His Son. This was to give them their natural being, bestowing upon them many graces and natural gifts, making them perfect, as it is written in the book of Genesis: "God saw all the things that He had made: and they were very good." [74] To see all things very good was to make them very good in the Word, His Son. He not only gave them their being and their natural graces when He beheld them, but He also clothed them with beauty in the face of His Son, communicating to them a supernatural being when He made man, and exalted him to the beauty of God, and, by consequence, all creatures in him, because He united Himself to the nature of them all in man. For this cause the Son of God Himself said, "And I, if I be lifted up from the earth will draw all things to Myself." [75] And thus in this exaltation of the incarnation of His Son, and the glory of His resurrection according to the flesh, the Father not only made all things beautiful in part, but also, we may well say, clothed them wholly with beauty and dignity.

A Spiritual Canticle of the Soul and the Bridegroom Christ

NOTE

BUT beyond all this -- speaking now of contemplation as it affects the soul and makes an impression on it -- in the vivid contemplation and knowledge of created things the soul beholds such a multiplicity of graces, powers, and beauty with which God has endowed them, that they seem to it to be clothed with admirable beauty and supernatural virtue derived from the infinite supernatural beauty of the face of God, whose beholding of them clothed the heavens and the earth with beauty and joy; as it is written: "You open Your hand and fill with blessing every living creature." [76] Hence the soul wounded with love of that beauty of the Beloved which it traces in created things, and anxious to behold that beauty which is the source of this visible beauty, sings as in the following stanza:

Footnotes:

73. Heb. 1:3
74. Gen. 1:31
75. John 12:32
76. Ps. 144:16

STANZA VI

THE BRIDE

> Oh! who can heal me?
> Give me perfectly Yourself,
> Send me no more
> A messenger
> Who cannot tell me what I wish.

AS created things furnish to the soul traces of the Beloved, and exhibit the impress of His beauty and magnificence, the love of the soul increases, and consequently the pain of His absence: for the greater the soul's knowledge of God the greater its desire to see Him, and its pain when it cannot; and as it sees there is no remedy for this pain except in the presence and vision of the Beloved, distrustful of every other remedy, it prays in this stanza for the fruition of His presence, saying: "Entertain me no more with any knowledge or communications or impressions of Your grandeur, for these do but increase my longing and the pain of Your absence; Your presence alone can satisfy my will and desire." The will cannot be satisfied with anything less than the vision of God, and therefore the soul prays that He may be pleased to give Himself to it in truth, in perfect love.

"O! who can heal me?"

2. That is, there is nothing in all the delights of the world, nothing in the satisfaction of the senses, nothing in the sweet taste of the spirit that can heal or content me, and therefore it adds:

"Give me at once Yourself."

3. No soul that really loves can be satisfied or content short of the fruition of God. For everything else, as I have just said, not only does not satisfy the soul, but rather increases the hunger and thirst of seeing Him as He us. Thus every glimpse of the Beloved, every knowledge and impression or communication from Him -- these are the messengers suggestive of Him -- increase and quicken the soul's desire after Him, as crumbs of food in hunger stimulate the appetite. The soul, therefore, mourning over the misery of being entertained by matters of so little moment, cries out:

"Give me perfectly Yourself."

4. Now all our knowledge of God in this life, however great it may be, is not a perfectly true knowledge of Him, because it is partial and incomplete; but to know Him essentially is true knowledge, and that is it which the soul prays for here, not satisfied with any other kind. Hence it says:

"Send me no more a messenger."

5. That is, grant that I may no longer know You in this imperfect way by the messengers of knowledge and impressions, which are so distant from that which my soul desires; for these messengers, as You well know, O my Bridegroom, do but increase the pain of Your absence. They renew the wound which You have inflicted by the knowledge of You which they convey, and they seem to delay Your coming. Henceforth send me no more of these inadequate communications, for if I have been hitherto satisfied with them, it was owing to the slightness of my knowledge and of my love: now that my love has become great, I cannot satisfy myself with them; therefore, give me at once Yourself.

6. This, more clearly expressed, is as follows: "O Lord my Bridegroom, Who gave me Yourself partially before, give me Yourself wholly now. You who showed glimpses of Yourself before, show Yourself clearly now. You who communicated Yourself hitherto by the instrumentality of messengers -- it was as if You mocked me -- give Yourself by Yourself now. Sometimes when You visited me You

A Spiritual Canticle of the Soul and the Bridegroom Christ
gave me the pearl of Your possession, and, when I began to examine it, lo, it was gone, for You had hidden it Yourself: it was like a mockery. Give me then Yourself in truth, Your whole self, that I may have You wholly to myself wholly, and send me no messengers again."

"Who cannot tell me what I wish."

7. "I wish for You wholly, and Your messengers neither know You wholly, nor can they speak of You wholly, for there is nothing in earth or heaven that can furnish that knowledge to the soul which it longs for. They cannot tell me, therefore, what I wish. Instead, then, of these messengers, be You the messenger and the message."

STANZA VII

All they who serve are telling me
Of Your unnumbered graces;
And all wound me more and more,
And something leaves me dying,
I know not what, of which they are darkly speaking.

THE soul describes itself in the foregoing stanza as wounded, or sick with love of the Bridegroom, because of the knowledge of Him which the irrational creation supplies, and in the present, as wounded with love because of the other and higher knowledge which it derives from the rational creation, nobler than the former; that is, angels and men. This is not all, for the soul says also that it is dying of love, because of that marvelous immensity not wholly but partially revealed to it through the rational creation. This it calls "I know not what," because it cannot be described, and because it is such that the soul dies of it.

2. It seems, from this, that there are three kinds of pain in the soul's love of the Beloved, corresponding to the three kinds of knowledge that can be had of Him. The first is called a wound; not deep, but slight, like a wound which heals quickly, because it comes from its knowledge of the creatures, which are the lowest works of God. This wounding of the soul, called also sickness, is thus spoken of by the bride in the Canticle: "I adjure you, O daughters of Jerusalem, if you find my Beloved, that you tell Him that I languish with love." [77] The daughters of Jerusalem are the creatures.

3. The second is called a sore which enters deeper than a wound into the soul, and is, therefore, of longer continuance, because it is as a wound festering, on account of which the soul feels that it is really dying of love. This sore is the effect of the knowledge of the works of God, the incarnation of the Word, and the mysteries of the faith. These being the greatest works of God, and involving a greater love than those of creation, produce a greater effect of love in the soul. If the first kind of pain is as a wound, this must be like a festering, continuous sore. Of this speaks the Bridegroom, addressing Himself to the bride, saying: "You have wounded My heart, My sister, My bride; you have wounded My heart with one of your eyes, and with one hair of your neck." [78] The eye signifies faith in the incarnation of the Bridegroom, and the one hair is the love of the same.

4. The third kind of pain is like dying; it is as if the whole soul were festering because of its wound. It is dying a living death until love, having slain it, shall make it live the life of love, transforming it in love. This dying of love is affected by a single touch of the knowledge of the Divinity; it is the "I know not what," of which the creatures, as in the stanza is said, are speaking indistinctly. This touch is not continuous nor great, -- for then soul and body would part -- but soon over, and thus the soul is dying of love, and dying the more when it sees that it cannot die of love. [79] This is called impatient love, which is spoken of in the book of Genesis, where the Scripture says that Rachel's love of children was so great that she said to Jacob her husband, "Give me children, otherwise I shall die." [80] And the prophet Job said, "Who will grant that . . . He that has begun the same would cut me off." [81]

5. These two-fold pains of love -- that is, the wound and the dying -- are in the stanza said to be merely the rational creation. The wound, when it speaks of the unnumbered graces of the Beloved in the mysteries and wisdom of God taught by the faith. The dying, when it is said that the rational creation speaks indistinctly. This is a sense and knowledge of the Divinity sometimes revealed when the soul hears God spoken of. Therefore it says:

"All they who serve."

6. That is, the rational creation, angels and men; for these alone are they who serve God, understanding by that word intelligent service; that is to say, all they who serve God. Some serve Him by contemplation and fruition in heaven -- these are the angels; others by loving and longing for Him on earth -- these are men. And because the soul learns to know God more distinctly through the rational creation, whether by considering its superiority over the rest of creation, or by what it teaches us of God -- the angels interiorly by secret inspirations, and men exteriorly by the truths of Scripture -- it says:

A Spiritual Canticle of the Soul and the Bridegroom Christ
"Telling me of Your unnumbered graces."

7. That is, they speak of the wonders of Your grace and mercy in the Incarnation, and in the truths of the faith which they show forth and are ever telling more distinctly; for the more they say, the more do they reveal Your graces.

"And all wound me more and more."

8. The more the angels inspire me, the more men teach me, the more do I love You; and thus all wound me more and more with love.

"And something leaves me dying, I know not what, of which they are darkly speaking."

9. It is as if it said: "But beside the wound which the creatures inflict when they tell me of Your unnumbered graces, there is yet something which remains to be told, one thing unknown to be uttered, a most clear trace of the footsteps of God revealed to the soul, which it should follow, a most profound knowledge of God, which is ineffable, and therefore spoken of as I know not what.'" If that which I comprehend inflicts the wound and festering sore of love, that which I cannot comprehend but yet feel profoundly, kills me.

10. This happens occasionally to souls advanced, whom God favors in what they hear, or see, or understand -- and sometimes without these or other means -- with a certain profound knowledge, in which they feel or apprehend the greatness and majesty of God. In this state they think so highly of God as to see clearly that they know Him not, and in their perception of His greatness they recognize that not to comprehend Him is the highest comprehension. And thus, one of the greatest favors of God, bestowed transiently on the soul in this life, is to enable it to see so distinctly, and to feel so profoundly, that it clearly understands it cannot comprehend Him at all. These souls are herein, in some degree, like the saints in heaven, where they who know Him most perfectly perceive most clearly that He is infinitely incomprehensible, for those who have the less clear vision, do not perceive so distinctly as the others, how greatly He transcends their vision. This is clear to none who have not had experience of it. But the experienced soul, comprehending that there is something further of which it is profoundly sensible, calls it, "I know not what." As that cannot be understood, so neither can it be described, though it is felt, as I have said. Hence the soul says that the creatures speak indistinctly, because they cannot distinctly utter that which they would say: it is the speech of infants, who cannot explain distinctly or speak intelligibly that which they would convey to others.

11. The other creatures, also, are in some measure a revelation to the soul in this way, but not of an order so high, whenever it is the good pleasure of God to manifest to it their spiritual sense and significance; they are seemingly on the point of making us understand the perfections of God, and cannot compass it; it is as if one were about to explain a matter and the explanation is not given; and thus they stammer "I know not what." The soul continues to complain, and addresses its own life, saying, in the stanza that follows:

Footnotes:

77. Cant. 5:8
78. Cant. 4:9
79. See Living Flame,' stanza 3, line 3, sect. 20.
80. Gen. 30:1
81. Job 6:8, 9

St. John of the Cross

STANZA VIII

But how you persevere, O life!
Not living where you live;
The arrows bring death
Which you receive
From your conceptions of the Beloved.

THE soul, perceiving itself to be dying of love, as it has just said, and yet not dying so as to have the free enjoyment of its love, complains of the continuance of its bodily life, by which the spiritual life is delayed. Here the soul addresses itself to the life it is living upon earth, magnifying the sorrows of it. The meaning of the stanza therefore is as follows: "O life of my soul, how can you persevere in this life of the flesh, seeing that it is your death and the privation of the true spiritual life in God, in Whom you live in substance, love, and desire, more truly than in the body? And if this were not reason enough to depart, and free yourself from the body of this death, so as to live and enjoy the life of God, how can you still remain in a body so frail? Besides, these wounds of love made by the Beloved in the revelation of His majesty are by themselves alone sufficient to put an end to your life, for they are very deep; and thus all your feelings towards Him, and all you know of Him, are so many touches and wounds of love that kill,

"But how you persevere, O life! Not living where you live."

2. We must keep in mind, for the better understanding of this, that the soul lives there where it loves, rather than in the body which it animates. The soul does not live by the body, but, on the contrary, gives it life, and lives by love in that which it loves. For beside this life of love which it lives in God Who loves it, the soul has its radical and natural life in God, like all created things, according to the saying of St. Paul: "In Him we live, and move, and are;"[82] that is, our life, motion, and being is in God. St. John also says that all that was made was life in God: "That which was made, in Him was life."[83]

3. When the soul sees that its natural life is in God through the being He has given it, and its spiritual life also because of the love it bears Him, it breaks forth into lamentations, complaining that so frail a life in a mortal body should have the power to hinder it from the fruition of the true, real, and delicious life, which it lives in God by nature and by love. Earnestly, therefore, does the soul insist upon this: it tells us that it suffers between two contradictions -- its natural life in the body, and its spiritual life in God; contrary the one to the other, because of their mutual repugnance. The soul living this double life is of necessity in great pain; for the painful life hinders the delicious, so that the natural life is as death, seeing that it deprives the soul of its spiritual life, wherein is its whole being and life by nature, and all its operations and feelings by love. The soul, therefore, to depict more vividly the hardships of this fragile life, says:

"The arrows bring death which you receive."

4. That is to say: "Besides, how can you continue in the body, seeing that the touches of love -- these are the arrows -- with which the Beloved pierces your heart, are alone sufficient to deprive you of life?" These touches of love make the soul and heart so fruitful of the knowledge and love of God, that they may well be called conceptions of God, as in the words that follow:

"From your conceptions of the Beloved."

5. That is, of the majesty, beauty, wisdom, grace, and power, which you know to be His.

A Spiritual Canticle of the Soul and the Bridegroom Christ
NOTE

AS the hart wounded with a poisoned arrow cannot be easy and at rest, but seeks relief on all sides, plunging into the waters here and again there, while the poison spreads notwithstanding all attempts at relief, till it reaches the heart, and occasions death; so the soul, pierced by the arrow of love, never ceases from seeking to alleviate its pains. Not only does it not succeed, but its pains increase, let it think, say, and do what it may; and knowing this, and that there is no other remedy but the resignation of itself into the hands of Him Who wounded it, that He may relieve it, and effectually slay it through the violence of its love; it turns towards the Bridegroom, Who is the cause of all, and says:

Footnotes:

82. Acts 17:28

83. John 1:3. The Saint adopts an old punctuation, different from the usual one. He reads thus: Omnia per Ipsum facta sunt, et sine Ipso factum est nihil: Quod factum est, in Ipso vita erat' (All things were made by Him, and without Him nothing was made: What was made in Him was life').

STANZA IX

Why, after wounding
This heart, have You not healed it?
And why, after stealing it,
Have You thus abandoned it,
And not carried away the stolen prey?

HERE the soul returns to the Beloved, still complaining of its pain; for that impatient love which the soul now exhibits admits of no rest or cessation from pain; so it sets forth its griefs in all manner of ways until it finds relief. The soul seeing itself wounded and lonely, and as no one can heal it but the Beloved Who has wounded it, asks why He, having wounded its heart with that love which the knowledge of Him brings, does not heal it in the vision of His presence; and why He thus abandons the heart which He has stolen through the love Which inflames it, after having deprived the soul of all power over it. The soul has now no power over its heart -- for he who loves has none -- because it is surrendered to the Beloved, and yet He has not taken it to Himself in the pure and perfect transformation of love in glory.

"Why, after wounding this heart, have You not healed it?"

2. The enamored soul is complaining not because it is wounded, for the deeper the wound the greater the joy, but because, being wounded, it is not healed by being wounded to death. The wounds of love are so deliciously sweet, that if they do not kill, they cannot satisfy the soul. They are so sweet that it desires to die of them, and hence it is that it says, "Why, after wounding this heart, have You not healed it?" That is, "Why have You struck it so sharply as to wound it so deeply, and yet not healed it by killing it utterly with love? As You are the cause of its pain in the affliction of love, be You also the cause of its health by a death from love; so the heart, wounded by the pain of Your absence, shall be healed in the delight and glory of Your Sweet presence." Therefore it goes on:

"And why, after stealing it, have You thus abandoned it?"

3. Stealing is nothing else but the act of a robber in dispossessing the owner of his goods, and possessing them himself. Here the soul complains to the Beloved that He has robbed it of its heart lovingly, and taken it out of its power and possession, and then abandoned it, without taking it into His own power and possession as the thief does with the goods he steals, carrying them away with him. He who is in love is said to have lost his heart, or to have it stolen by the object of his love; because it is no longer in his own possession, but in the power of the object of his love, and so his heart is not his own, but the property of the person he loves.

4. This consideration will enable the soul to determine whether it loves God simply or not. If it loves Him it will have no heart for itself, nor for its own pleasure or profit, but for the honor, glory, and pleasure of God; because the more the heart is occupied with self, the less is it occupied with God. Whether God has really stolen the heart, the soul may ascertain by either of these two signs: Is it anxiously seeking after God? and has it no pleasure in anything but in Him, as the soul here says? The reason of this is that the heart cannot rest in peace without the possession of something; and when its affections are once placed, it has neither the possession of itself nor of anything else; neither does it perfectly possess what it loves. In this state its weariness is in proportion to its loss, until it shall enter into possession and be satisfied; for until then the soul is as an empty vessel waiting to be filled, as a hungry man eager for food, as a sick man sighing for health, and as a man suspended in the air.

"And not carried away the stolen prey?"

5. "Why do You not carry away the heart which Your love has stolen, to fill it, to heal it, and to satiate it giving it perfect rest in Yourself?"
6. The loving soul, for the sake of greater conformity with the Beloved, cannot cease to desire the

A Spiritual Canticle of the Soul and the Bridegroom Christ

recompense and reward of its love for the sake of which it serves the Beloved, otherwise it could not be true love, for the recompense of love is nothing else, and the soul seeks nothing else, but greater love, until it reaches the perfection of love; for the sole reward of love is love, as we learn from the prophet Job, who, speaking of his own distress, which is that of the soul now referred to, says: "As a servant longs for the shade, as the hireling looks for the end of his work; so I also have had empty months, and have numbered to myself wearisome nights. If I sleep, I say, When shall I arise? and again, I shall look for the evening, and shall be filled with sorrows even till darkness." [84]

7. Thus, then, the soul on fire with the love of God longs for the perfection and consummation of its love, that it may be completely refreshed. As the servant wearied by the heat of the day longs for the cooling shade, and as the hireling looks for the end of his work, so the soul for the end of its own. Observe, Job does not say that the hireling looks for the end of his labor, but only for the end of his work. He teaches us that the soul which loves looks not for the end of its labor, but for the end of its work; because its work is to love, and it is the end of this work, which is love, that it hopes for, namely, the perfect love of God. Until it attains to this, the words of Job will be always true of it -- its months will be empty, and its nights wearisome and tedious. It is clear, then, that the soul which loves God seeks and looks for no other reward of its services than to love God perfectly.

NOTE

THE soul, having reached this degree of love, resembles a sick man exceedingly wearied, whose appetite is gone, and to whom his food is loathsome, and all things annoyance and trouble. Amidst all things that present themselves to his thoughts, or feelings, or sight, his only wish and desire is health; and everything that does not contribute to it is weariness and oppressive. The soul, therefore, in pain because of its love of God, has three peculiarities. Under all circumstances, and in all affairs, the thought of its health -- that is, the Beloved -- is ever present to it; and though it is obliged to attend to them because it cannot help it, its heart is ever with Him. The second peculiarity, namely, a loss of pleasure in everything, arises from the first. The third also, a consequence of the second, is that all things become wearisome, and all affairs full of vexation and annoyance.

2. The reason is that the palate of the will having touched and tasted of the food of the love of God, the will instantly, under all circumstances, regardless of every other consideration, seeks the fruition of the Beloved. It is with the soul now as it was with Mary Magdalene, when in her burning love she sought Him in the garden. She, thinking Him to be the gardener, spoke to Him without further reflection, saying: "If you have taken Him hence, tell me where you have laid Him, and I will take Him away." [85] The soul is under the influence of a like anxiety to find Him in all things, and not finding Him immediately, as it desires -- but rather the very reverse -- not only has no pleasure in them, but is even tormented by them, and sometimes exceedingly so: for such souls suffer greatly in their intercourse with men and in the transactions of the world, because these things hinder rather than help them in their search.

3. The bride in the Canticle shows us that she had these three peculiarities when seeking the Bridegroom. "I sought Him and found Him not; the keepers that go about the city found me, they struck me and wounded me: the keepers of the walls took away my cloak." [86] The keepers that go about the city are the affairs of this world, which, when they "find" a soul seeking after God, inflict upon it much pain, and grief, and loathing; for the soul not only does not find in them what it seeks, but rather a hindrance. They who keep the wall of contemplation, that the soul may not enter -- that is, evil spirits and worldly affairs -- take away the cloak of peace and the quiet of loving contemplation. All this inflicts infinite vexation on the soul enamored of God; and while it remains on earth without the vision of God, there is no relief, great or small, from these afflictions, and the soul therefore continues to complain to the Beloved, saying:

Footnotes:

84. Job 7:2-4
85. John 20:15
86. Cant. 6:6, 7

STANZA X

Quench my troubles,
For no one else can soothe them;
And let my eyes behold You,
For You are their light,
And I will keep them for You alone.

HERE the soul continues to beseech the Beloved to put an end to its anxieties and distress -- none other than He can do so -- and that in such a way that its eyes may behold Him; for He alone is the light by which they see, and there is none other but He on whom it will look.

"Quench my troubles."

2. The desire of love has this property, that everything said or done which does not become that which the will loves, wearies and annoys it, and makes it peevish when it sees itself disappointed in its desires. This and its weary longing after the vision of God is here called "troubles." These troubles nothing can remove except the possession of the Beloved; hence the soul prays Him to quench them with His presence, to cool their feverishness, as the cooling water him who is wearied by the heat. The soul makes use of the expression "quench," to denote its sufferings from the fire of love.

"For no one else can soothe them."

3. The soul, in order to move and persuade the Beloved to grant its petition, says, "As none other but You can satisfy my needs, You quench my troubles." Remember here that God is then close at hand, to comfort the soul and to satisfy its wants, when it has and seeks no satisfaction or comfort out of Him. The soul that finds no pleasure out of God cannot be long unvisited by the Beloved.

"And let my eyes behold You."

4. Let me see You face to face with the eyes of the soul,

"For you are their light."

5. God is the supernatural light of the soul, without which it abides in darkness. And now, in the excess of its affection, it calls Him the light of its eyes, as an earthly lover, to express his affection, calls the object of his love the light of his eyes. The soul says in effect in the foregoing terms, "Since my eyes have no other light, either of nature or of love, but You, let them behold You, Who in every way are their light." David was regretting this light when he said in his trouble, "The light of my eyes, and the same is not with me;" [87] and Tobit, when he said, "What manner of joy shall be to me who sit in darkness, and see not the light of heaven?" [88] He was longing for the clear vision of God; for the light of heaven is the Son of God; as St. John says in the Revelation: "And the city needs not sun, nor moon to shine in it; for the glory of God has illuminated it, and the Lamb is the lamp thereof." [89]

"And I will keep them for You alone."

6. The soul seeks to constrain the Bridegroom to let it see the light of its eyes, not only because it would be in darkness without it, but also because it will not look upon anything but on Him. For as that soul is justly deprived of this divine light if it fixes the eyes of the will on any other light, proceeding from anything that is not God, for then its vision is confined to that object; so also the soul, by a certain fitness, deserves the divine light, if it shuts its eyes against all objects whatever, to open them only for the vision of God.

A Spiritual Canticle of the Soul and the Bridegroom Christ
NOTE

BUT the loving Bridegroom of souls cannot bear to see them suffer long in the isolation of which I am speaking, for, as He says by the mouth of Zachariah, "He that shall touch you, touches the apple of My eye;" [90] especially when their sufferings, as those of this soul, proceed from their love for Him. Therefore does He speak through Isaiah, "It shall be before they call, I will hear; as they are yet speaking, I will hear." [91] And the wise man says that the soul that seeks Him as treasure shall find Him. [92] God grants a certain spiritual presence of Himself to the fervent prayers of the loving soul which seeks Him more earnestly than treasure, seeing that it has abandoned all things, and even itself, for His sake.

2. In that presence He shows certain profound glimpses of His divinity and beauty, whereby He still increases the soul's anxious desire to behold Him. For as men throw water on the coals of the forge to cause intenser heat, so our Lord in His dealings with certain souls, in the intermission of their love, makes some revelations of His majesty, to quicken their fervor, and to prepare them more and more for those graces which He will give them afterwards. Thus the soul, in that obscure presence of God, beholding and feeling the supreme good and beauty hidden there, is dying in desire of the vision, saying in the stanza that follows:

Footnotes:

87. Ps. 37:11
88. Tob. 5:12
89. Rev. 21:23
90. Zech. 2:8
91. Isa. 65:24
92. Prov. 2:4, 5

St. John of the Cross

STANZA XI

Reveal Your presence,
And let the vision and Your beauty kill me.
Behold the malady
Of love is incurable
Except in Your presence and before Your face.

THE soul, anxious to be possessed by God, Who is so great, Whose love has wounded and stolen its heart, and unable to suffer more, beseeches Him directly, in this stanza, to reveal His beauty -- that is, the divine Essence -- and to slay it in that vision, separating it from the body, in which it can neither see nor possess Him as it desires. And further, setting before Him the distress and sorrow of heart, in which it continues, suffering it because of its love, and unable to find any other remedy than the glorious vision of the divine essence, cries out: "Reveal Your presence."

2. To understand this clearly we must remember that there are three ways in which God is present in the soul. The first is His presence in essence, not in holy souls only, but in wretched and sinful souls as well, and also in all created things; for it is by this presence that He gives life and being, and were it once withdrawn all things would return to nothing. [93] This presence never fails in the soul.

3. The second is His presence by grace, whereby He dwells in the soul, pleased and satisfied with it. This presence is not in all souls; for those who fall into mortal sin lose it, and no soul can know in a natural way whether it has it or not. The third is His presence by spiritual affection. God is wont to show His presence in many devout souls in diverse ways, in refreshment, joy, and gladness; yet this, like the others, is all secret, for He does not show Himself as He is, because the condition of our mortal life does not admit of it. Thus this prayer of the soul may be understood of any one of them.

"Reveal Your presence."

4. Inasmuch as it is certain that God is ever present in the soul, at least in the first way, the soul does not say, "Be present"; but, "Reveal and manifest Your hidden presence, whether natural, spiritual, or affective, in such a way that I may behold You in Your divine essence and beauty." The soul prays Him that as He by His essential presence gives it its natural being, and perfects it by His presence of grace, so also He would glorify it by the manifestation of His glory. But as the soul is now loving God with fervent affections, the presence, for the revelation of which it prays the Beloved to manifest, is to be understood chiefly of the affective presence of the Beloved. Such is the nature of this presence that the soul felt there was an infinite being hidden there, out of which God communicated to it certain obscure visions of His own divine beauty. Such was the effect of these visions that the soul longed and fainted away with the desire of that which is hidden in that presence.

5. This is in harmony with the experience of David, when he said: "My soul longs and faints for the courts of our Lord." [94] The soul now faints with desire of being absorbed in the Sovereign Good which it feels to be present and hidden; for though it is hidden, the soul is most profoundly conscious of the good and delight which are there. The soul is therefore attracted to this good with more violence than matter is to its center, and is unable to contain itself, by reason of the force of this attraction, from saying:

"Reveal Your presence."

6. Moses, on Mount Sinai in the presence of God, saw such glimpses of the majesty and beauty of His hidden Divinity, that, unable to endure it, he prayed twice for the vision of His glory saying: "Whereas You have said: I know you by name, and you have found grace in my sight. If, therefore, I have found grace in Your sight, show me Your face, that I may know You and may find grace before Your eyes;" [95] that is, the grace which he longed for -- to attain to the perfect love of the glory of God. The answer of our Lord was: "You can not see My face, for man shall not see Me and live." [96] It is as if God had said: "Moses, your prayer is difficult to grant; the beauty of My face, and the joy in seeing Me is so great, as to be more than your soul can bear in a mortal body that is so weak." The soul

A Spiritual Canticle of the Soul and the Bridegroom Christ

accordingly, conscious of this truth, either because of the answer made to Moses or also because of that which I spoke of before, [97] namely, the feeling that there is something still in the presence of God here which it could not see in its beauty in the life it is now living, because, as I said before, [98] it faints when it sees but a glimpse of it. Hence it comes that it anticipates the answer that may be given to it, as it was to Moses, and says:

"Let the vision and Your beauty kill me."

7. That is, "Since the vision of You and Your beauty is so full of delight that I cannot endure, but must die in the act of beholding them, let the vision and Your beauty kill me."

8. Two visions are said to be fatal to man, because he cannot bear them and live. One, that of the basilisk, at the sight of which men are said to die at once. The other is the vision of God; but there is a great difference between them. The former kills by poison, the other with infinite health and bliss. It is, therefore, nothing strange for the soul to desire to die by beholding the beauty of God in order to enjoy Him for ever. If the soul had but one single glimpse of the majesty and beauty of God, not only would it desire to die once in order to see Him for ever, as it desires now, but would most joyfully undergo a thousand most bitter deaths to see Him even for a moment, and having seen Him would suffer as many deaths again to see Him for another moment.

9. It is necessary to observe for the better explanation of this line, that the soul is now speaking conditionally, when it prays that the vision and beauty may slay it; it assumes that the vision must be preceded by death, for if it were possible before death, the soul would not pray for death, because the desire of death is a natural imperfection. The soul, therefore, takes it for granted that this corruptible life cannot coexist with the incorruptible life of God, and says:

"Let the vision and Your beauty kill me."

10. St. Paul teaches this doctrine to the Corinthians when he says: "We would not be spoiled, but overclothed, that that which is mortal may be swallowed up of life," [99] That is, "we would not be divested of the flesh, but invested with glory." But reflecting that he could not live in glory and in a mortal body at the same time, he says to the Philippians: "having a desire to be dissolved and to be with Christ." [100]

11. Here arises this question, Why did the people of Israel of old dread and avoid the vision of God, that they might not die, as it appears they did from the words of Manoah to his wife, "We shall die because we have seen God," [101] when the soul desires to die of that vision? To this question two answers may be given.

12. In those days men could not see God, though dying in the state of grace, because Christ had not come. It was therefore more profitable for them to live in the flesh, increasing in merit, and enjoying their natural life, than to be in Limbo, incapable of meriting, suffering in the darkness and in the spiritual absence of God. They therefore considered it a great grace and blessing to live long upon earth.

13. The second answer is founded on considerations drawn from the love of God. They in those days, not being so confirmed in love, nor so near to God by love, were afraid of the vision: but, now, under the law of grace, when, on the death of the body, the soul may behold God, it is more profitable to live but a short time, and then to die in order to see Him. And even if the vision were withheld, the soul that really loves God will not be afraid to die at the sight of Him; for true love accepts with perfect resignation, and in the same spirit, and even with joy, whatever comes to it from the hands of the Beloved, whether prosperity or adversity -- yes, and even chastisements such as He shall be pleased to send, for, as St. John says, "perfect charity casts out fear." [102]

14. Thus, then, there is no bitterness in death to the soul that loves, when it brings with it all the sweetness and delights of love; there is no sadness in the remembrance of it when it opens the door to all joy; nor can it be painful and oppressive, when it is the end of all unhappiness and sorrow, and the beginning of all good. Yes, the soul looks upon it as a friend and its bride, and exults in the recollection of it as the day of espousals; it yearns for the day and hour of death more than the kings of the earth for principalities and kingdoms.

15. It was of this kind of death that the wise man said, "O death, your judgment is good to the needy man." [103] If it is good to the needy man, though it does not supply his wants, but on the contrary deprives him even of what he has, how much more good will it be to the soul in need of love and which is crying for more, when it will not only not rob it of the love it has already, but will be the occasion of that fullness of love which it yearns for, and is the supply of all its necessities. It is not without reason, then, that the soul ventures to say:

"Let the vision and Your beauty kill me."

St. John of the Cross

16. The soul knows well that in the instant of that vision it will be itself absorbed and transformed into that beauty, and be made beautiful like it, enriched, and abounding in beauty as that beauty itself. This is why David said, "Precious in the sight of the Lord is the death of His saints," [104] but that could not be if they did not become partakers of His glory, for there is nothing precious in the eyes of God except that which He is Himself, and therefore, the soul, when it loves, fears not death, but rather desires it. But the sinner is always afraid to die, because he suspects that death will deprive him of all good, and inflict upon him all evil; for in the words of David, "the death of the wicked is very evil," [105] and therefore, as the wise man says, the very thought of it is bitter: "O death, how bitter is your memory to a man that has peace in his riches!" [106] The wicked love this life greatly, and the next but little, and are therefore afraid of death; but the soul that loves God lives more in the next life than in this, because it lives rather where it loves than where it dwells, and therefore esteeming but lightly its present bodily life, cries out: "Let the vision and Your beauty kill me."

"Behold, the malady of love is incurable, except in Your presence and before Your face."

17. The reason why the malady of love admits of no other remedy than the presence and countenance of the Beloved is that the malady of love differs from every other sickness, and therefore requires a different remedy. In other diseases, according to sound philosophy, contraries are cured by contraries; but love is not cured but by that which is in harmony with itself. The reason is that the health of the soul consists in the love of God; and so when that love is not perfect, its health is not perfect, and the soul is therefore sick, for sickness is nothing else but a failure of health. Thus, that soul which loves not at all is dead; but when it loves a little, however little that may be, it is then alive, though exceedingly weak and sick because it loves God so little. But the more its love increases, the greater will be its health, and when its love is perfect, then, too, its health also is perfect. Love is not perfect until the lovers become so on an equality as to be mutually transformed into one another; then love is wholly perfect.

18. And because the soul is now conscious of a certain adumbration of love, which is the malady of which it here speaks, yearning to be made like to Him of whom it is a shadow, that is the Bridegroom, the Word, the Son of God, Who, as St. Paul says, is the "splendor of His glory, and the figure of His substance;" [107] and because it is into this figure it desires to be transformed by love, cries out, "Behold, the malady of love is incurable except in Your presence, and in the light of Your Countenance." The love that is imperfect is rightly called a malady, because as a sick man is enfeebled and cannot work, so the soul that is weak in love is also enfeebled and cannot practice heroic virtue.

19. Another explanation of these words is this: he who feels this malady of love -- that is, a failure of it -- has an evidence in himself that he has some love, because he ascertains what is deficient in him by that which he possesses. But he who is not conscious of this malady has evidence therein that he has no love at all, or that he has already attained to perfect love.

NOTE

THE soul now conscious of a vehement longing after God, like a stone rushing to its center, and like wax which has begun to receive the impression of the seal which it cannot perfectly represent, and knowing, moreover, that it is like a picture lightly sketched, crying for the artist to finish his work, and having its faith so clear as to trace most distinctly certain divine glimpses of the majesty of God, knows not what else to do but to turn inward to that faith -- as involving and veiling the face and beauty of the Beloved -- from which it has received those impressions and pledges of love, and which it thus addresses:

Footnotes:

93. See Ascent of Mount Carmel,' bk. 2, ch. 5, sect. 3.
94. Ps. 83:3
95. Exod. 33:12, 13
96. Exod. 33:20
97. Stan. vii. sect. 10.
98. Above, sect. 4.
99. 2 Cor. 5:4
100. Phil. 1:23
101. Judg. 13:22
102. 1 John 4:18
103. Ecclus. 41:3
104. Ps. 115:15

A Spiritual Canticle of the Soul and the Bridegroom Christ
    105. Ps. 33:22
    106. Ecclus. 41:1
    107. Heb. 1:3

STANZA XII

O crystal well!
O that on Your silvered surface
You would mirror forth at once
Those desired eyes
Which are outlined in my heart.

THE soul vehemently desiring to be united to the Bridegroom, and seeing that there is no help or succor in created things, turns towards the faith, as to that which gives it the most vivid vision of the Beloved, and adopts it as the means to that end. And, indeed, there is no other way of attaining to true union, to the spiritual betrothal of God, according to the words of Hosea: "I will betrothe you to Me in faith." [108] In this fervent desire it cries out in the words of this stanza, which are in effect this: "O faith of Christ, my Bridegroom! Oh that you would manifest clearly those truths concerning the Beloved, secretly and obscurely infused -- for faith is, as theologians say, an obscure habit -- so that your informal and obscure communications may be in a moment clear; Oh that you would withdraw yourself formally and completely from these truths -- for faith is a veil over the truths of God -- and reveal them perfectly in glory." Accordingly it says:

"O crystal well!"

2. Faith is called crystal for two reasons: because it is of Christ the Bridegroom; because it has the property of crystal, pure in its truths, a limpid well clear of error, and of natural forms. It is a well because the waters of all spiritual goodness flow from it into the soul. Christ our Lord, speaking to the woman of Samaria, calls faith a well, saying, "The water that I will give him shall become in him a well of water springing up into life everlasting." [109] This water is the Spirit which they who believe shall receive by faith in Him. "Now this He said of the Spirit which they who believed in Him should receive." [110]

"Oh that on your silvered surface."

3. The articles and definitions of the faith are called silvered surfaces. In order to understand these words and those that follow, we must know that faith is compared to silver because of the propositions it teaches us, the truth and substance it involves being compared to gold. This very substance which we now believe, hidden behind the silver veil of faith, we shall clearly behold and enjoy hereafter; the gold of faith shall be made manifest. Hence the Psalmist, speaking of this, says: "If you sleep amidst the lots, the wings of the dove are laid over with silver, and the hinder parts of the back in the paleness of gold."[111] That means if we shall keep the eyes of the understanding from regarding the things of heaven and of earth -- this the Psalmist calls sleeping in the midst -- we shall be firm in the faith, here called dove, the wings of which are the truths laid over with silver, because in this life the faith puts these truths before us obscurely beneath a veil. This is the reason why the soul calls them silvered surface. But when faith shall have been consummated in the clear vision of God, then the substance of faith, the silver veil removed, will shine as gold.

4. As the faith gives and communicates to us God Himself, but hidden beneath the silver of faith, yet it reveals Him none the less. So if a man gives us a vessel made of gold, but covered with silver, he gives us in reality a vessel of gold, though the gold is covered over. Thus, when the bride in the Canticle was longing for the fruition of God, He promised it to her so far as the state of this life admitted of it, saying: "We will make you chains of gold inlaid with silver." [112] He thus promised to give Himself to her under the veil of faith. Hence the soul addresses the faith, saying: "Oh that on your silvered surface"-- the definitions of faith -- "in which you hide" the gold of the divine rays -- which are the desired eyes, -- instantly adding:

"You would mirror forth at once those desired eyes!"

A Spiritual Canticle of the Soul and the Bridegroom Christ

5. By the eyes are understood, as I have said, the rays and truths of God, which are set before us hidden and informal in the definitions of the faith. Thus the words say in substance: "Oh that you would formally and explicitly reveal to me those hidden truths which You teach implicitly and obscurely in the definitions of the faith; according to my earnest desire." Those truths are called eyes, because of the special presence of the Beloved, of which the soul is conscious, believing Him to be perpetually regarding it; and so it says:

"Which are outlined in my heart."

6. The soul here says that these truths are outlined in the heart -- that is, in the understanding and the will. It is through the understanding that these truths are infused into the soul by faith. They are said to be outlined because the knowledge of them is not perfect. As a sketch is not a perfect picture, so the knowledge that comes by faith is not a perfect understanding. The truths, therefore, infused into the soul by faith are as it were in outline, and when the clear vision shall be granted, then they will be as a perfect and finished picture, according to the words of the Apostle: "When that shall come which is perfect, that shall be made void which is in part." [113] "That which is perfect" is the clear vision, and "that which is in part" is the knowledge that comes by faith.

7. Besides this outline which comes by faith, there is another by love in the soul that loves -- that is, in the will -- in which the face of the Beloved is so deeply and vividly pictured, when the union of love occurs, that it may be truly said the Beloved lives in the loving soul, and the loving soul in the Beloved. Love produces such a resemblance by the transformation of those who love that one may be said to be the other, and both but one. The reason is, that in the union and transformation of love one gives himself up to the other as his possession, and each resigns, abandons, and exchanges himself for the other, and both become but one in the transformation wrought by love.

8. This is the meaning of St. Paul when he said, "I live, now, not I, but Christ lives in me." [114] In that He says, "I live, now, not I," his meaning is, that though he lived, yet the life he lived was not his own, because he was transformed in Christ: that his life was divine rather than human; and for that reason, he said it was not he that lived, but Christ Who lived in him. We may therefore say, according to this likeness of transformation, that his life and the life of Christ were one by the union of love. This will be perfect in heaven in the divine life of all those who shall merit the beatific vision; for, transformed in God, they will live the life of God and not their own, since the life of God will be theirs. Then they will say in truth. "We live, but not we ourselves, for God lives in us."

9. Now, this may take place in this life, as in the case of St. Paul, but not perfectly and completely, though the soul should attain to such a transformation of love as shall be spiritual marriage, which is the highest state it can reach in this life; because all this is but an outline of love compared with the perfect image of transformation in glory. Yet, when this outline of transformation is attained in this life, it is a grand blessing, because the Beloved is so greatly pleased therewith. He desires, therefore, that the bride should have Him thus delineated in her soul, and says to her, "Put Me as a seal upon your heart, as a seal upon your arm." [115] The heart here signifies the soul, wherein God in this life dwells as an impression of the seal of faith, and the arm is the resolute will, where He is as the impressed token of love.

10. Such is the state of the soul at that time. I speak but little of it, not willing to leave it altogether untouched, though no language can describe it.

11. The very substance of soul and body seems to be dried up by thirst after this living well of God, for the thirst resembles that of David when he cried out, "As the hart longs for the fountains of waters, so my soul longs for You, O God. My soul has thirsted after the strong living God; when shall I come and appear before the face of God?" [116] So oppressive is this thirst to the soul, that it counts it as nothing to break through the camp of the Philistines, like the valiant men of David, to fill its pitcher with "water out of the cisterns of Bethlehem," [117] which is Christ. The trials of this world, the rage of the devil, and the pains of hell are nothing to pass through, in order to plunge into this fathomless fountain of love.

12. To this we may apply those words in the Canticle: "Love is strong as death, jealousy is hard as hell." [118] It is incredible how vehement are the longings and sufferings of the soul when it sees itself on the point of testing this good, and at the same time sees it withheld; for the nearer the object desired, the greater the pangs of its denial: "Before I eat," says Job, "I sigh, and as it were overflowing waters so my roaring" [119] and hunger for food. God is meant here by food; for in proportion to the soul's longing for food, and its knowledge of God, is the pain it suffers now.

St. John of the Cross

NOTE

THE source of the grievous sufferings of the soul at this time is the consciousness of its own emptiness of God -- while it is drawing nearer and nearer to Him -- and also, the thick darkness with the spiritual fire, which dry and purify it, that, its purification ended, it may be united with God. For when God sends not forth a ray of supernatural light into the soul, He is to it intolerable darkness when He is even near to it in spirit, for the supernatural light by its very brightness obscures the mere natural light. David referred to this when he said: "Cloud and mist round about Him . . . a fire shall go before Him." [120] And again: "He put darkness His covert; His tabernacle is round about Him, darksome waters in the clouds of the air. Because of the brightness in His sight the clouds passed, hail and coals of fire." [121] The soul that approaches God feels Him to be all this more and more the further it advances, until He shall cause it to enter within His divine brightness through the transformation of love. But the comfort and consolations of God are, by His infinite goodness, proportional to the darkness and emptiness of the soul, as it is written, "As the darkness thereof, so also the light thereof."[122] And because He humbles souls and wearies them, while He is exalting them and making them glorious, He sends into the soul, in the midst of its weariness, certain divine rays from Himself, in such gloriousness and strength of love as to stir it up from its very depths, and to change its whole natural condition. Thus, the soul, in great fear and natural awe, addresses the Beloved in the first words of the following stanza, the remainder of which is His answer:

Footnotes:

108. Hos. 2:20
109. John 4:14
110. John 7:39
111. Ps. 67:14
112. Cant. 1:10
113. 1 Cor. 13:10
114. Gal. 2:20
115. Cant. 8:6
116. Ps. 41:1, 2
117. 1 Chr. 11:18
118. Cant. 8:6
119. Job 3:24
120. Ps. 96:2, 3
121. Ps. 17:12, 13
122. Ps. 138:12

STANZA XIII

Turn them away, O my Beloved!
I am on the Wing.

THE BRIDEGROOM

Return, My Dove!
The wounded hart
Looms on the hill
In the air of your flight and is refreshed.

EXPLANATION

AMID those fervent affections of love, such as the soul has shown in the preceding stanzas, the Beloved is wont to visit His bride, tenderly, lovingly, and with great strength of love; for ordinarily the graces and visits of God are great in proportion to the greatness of those fervors and longings of love which have gone before. And, as the soul has so anxiously longed for the divine eyes -- as in the foregoing stanza -- the Beloved reveals to it some glimpses of His majesty and Godhead, according to its desires. These divine rays strike the soul so profoundly and so vividly that it is rapt into an ecstasy which in the beginning is attended with great suffering and natural fear. Hence the soul, unable to bear the ecstasies in a body so frail, cries out, "Turn away your eyes from me."

"*Turn them away, O my Beloved!*"

2. That is, "Your divine eyes, for they make me fly away out of myself to the heights of contemplation, and my natural force cannot bear it." This the soul says because it thinks it has escaped from the burden of the flesh, which was the object of its desires; it therefore prays the Beloved to turn away His eyes; that is, not to show them in the body where it cannot bear and enjoy them as it would, but to show them to it in its flight from the body. The Bridegroom at once denies the request and hinders the flight, saying, "Return, My Dove! for the communications I make to you now are not those of the state of glory wherein you desire to be; but return to Me, for I am He Whom you, wounded with love, are seeking, and I, too, as the hart, wounded with your love, begin to show Myself to you on the heights of contemplation, and am refreshed and delighted by the love which your contemplation involves." The soul then says to the Bridegroom:

"*Turn them away, O my Beloved!*"

3. The soul, because of its intense longing after the divine eyes -- that is, the Godhead -- receives interiorly from the Beloved such communications and knowledge of God as compel it to cry out, "Turn them away, O my Beloved!" For such is the wretchedness of our mortal nature, that we cannot bear -- even when it is offered to us -- but at the cost of our life, that which is the very life of the soul, and the object of its earnest desires, namely, the knowledge of the Beloved. Thus the soul is compelled to say, with regard to the eyes so earnestly, so anxiously sought for, and in so many ways -- when they become visible -- "Turn them away."

4. So great, at times, is the suffering of the soul during these ecstatic visitations -- and there is no other pain which so wrenches the very bones, and which so oppresses our natural forces -- that, were it not for the special interference of God, death would ensue. And, in truth, such is it to the soul, the subject of these visitations, for it feels as if it were released from the body and a stranger to the flesh. Such graces cannot be perfectly received in the body, because the spirit of man is lifted up to the communion of the Spirit of God, Who visits the soul, and must therefore of necessity be in some measure a stranger to the body. Hence it is that the flesh has to suffer, and consequently the soul in it, by reason of their union in one person. The great agony of the soul, therefore, in these visitations, and the great fear that overwhelms it when God deals with it in the supernatural way, [123] force it to cry out,

St. John of the Cross

"Turn them away, O my Beloved!"

5. But it is not to be supposed, however, that the soul really wishes Him to turn away His eyes; for this is nothing else but the expression of natural awe, as I said before. [124] Yes, rather, cost they what they may, the soul would not willingly miss these visitations and favors of the Beloved; for though nature may suffer, the spirit flies to this supernatural recollection in order to enjoy the spirit of the Beloved, the object of its prayers and desires. The soul is unwilling to receive these visitations in the body, when it cannot have the perfect fruition of them, and only in a slight degree and in pain; but it covets them in the flight of the disembodied spirit when it can enjoy them freely. Hence it says, "Turn them away, my Beloved" -- that is, Do not visit me in the flesh.

"I am on the wing."

6. It is as if it said, "I am taking my flight out of the body, that You may show them when I shall have left it; they being the cause of my flight out of the body." For the better understanding of the nature of this flight we should consider that which I said just now. [125] In this visitation of the divine Spirit the spirit of the soul is with great violence borne upwards into communion with the divine, the body is abandoned, all its acts and senses are suspended, because they are absorbed in God. Thus the Apostle, St. Paul, speaking of his own ecstasy, says, "Whether in the body or out of the body, I cannot tell." [126] But we are not to suppose that the soul abandons the body, and that the natural life is destroyed, but only that its actions have then ceased.

7. This is the reason why the body remains insensible in raptures and ecstasies, and unconscious of the most painful inflictions. These are not like the swoons and faintings of the natural life, which cease when pain begins. They who have not arrived at perfection are liable to these visitations, for they happen to those who are walking in the way of proficients. They who are already perfect receive these visitations in peace and in the sweetness of love: ecstasies cease, for they were only graces to prepare them for this greater grace.

8. This is a fitting place for discussing the difference between raptures, ecstasies, other elevations and subtle flights of the spirit, to which spiritual persons are liable; but, as I intend to do nothing more than explain briefly this canticle, as I undertook in the prologue, I leave the subject for those who are better qualified than I am. I do this the more readily, because our mother, the blessed Teresa of Jesus, has written admirably on this matter, [127] whose writings I hope in God to see published soon. The flight of the soul in this place, then, is to be understood of ecstasy, and elevation of spirit in God. The Beloved immediately says:

"Return, My Dove."

9. The soul was joyfully quitting the body in its spiritual flight, thinking that its natural life was over, and that it was about to enter into the everlasting fruition of the Bridegroom, and remain with Him without a veil between them. He, however, restrains it in its flight, saying:

"Return, My Dove."

10. It is as if He said, "O My Dove, in your high and rapid flight of contemplation, in the love with which you are inflamed, in the simplicity of your regard" -- these are three characteristics of the dove -- "return from that flight in which you aim at the true fruition of Myself -- the time is not yet come for knowledge so high -- return, and submit yourself to that lower degree of it which I communicate in this your rapture."

"The wounded hart."

11. The Bridegroom likens Himself to a hart, for by the hart here He means Himself. The hart by nature climbs up to high places, and when wounded hastens to seek relief in the cooling waters. If he hears his consort moan and sees that she is wounded, he runs to her at once, comforts, and caresses her. So the Bridegroom now; for, seeing the bride wounded with His love, He, too, hearing her moaning, is wounded Himself with her love; for with lovers the wound of one is the wound of the other, and they have the same feelings in common. The Bridegroom, therefore, says in effect: "Return, my bride, to Me; for as you are wounded with the love of Me, I too, like the hart, am wounded by love for you. I am like the hart, looming on the top of the hill." Therefore He says:

"Looms on the hill."

A Spiritual Canticle of the Soul and the Bridegroom Christ

12. That is, "on the heights of contemplation, to which you have ascended in your flight." Contemplation is a lofty eminence where God, in this life, begins to communicate Himself to the soul, and to show Himself, but not distinctly. Hence it is said, "Looms on the hill," because He does not appear clearly. However profound the knowledge of Himself which God may grant to the soul in this life, it is, after all, but an indistinct vision. We now come to the third property of the hart, the subject of the line that follows:

"In the air of your flight, and is refreshed."

13. The flight is contemplation in the ecstasy spoken of before, [128] and the air is the spirit of love produced in the soul by this flight of contemplation, and this love produced by the flight is here with great propriety called "air," for the Holy Spirit also is likened to air in the Sacred Writings, because He is the breath of the Father and the Son. And so as He is there the air of the flight -- that is, that He proceeds by the will from the contemplation and wisdom of the Father and the Son, and is breathed -- so here the love of the soul is called air by the Bridegroom, because it proceeds from the contemplation of God and the knowledge of Him which at this time is possessed by the soul.

14. We must observe here that the Bridegroom does not say that He comes at the flight, but at the air of the flight, because properly speaking God does not communicate Himself to the soul because of that flight, which is, as I have said, the knowledge it has of God, but because of the love which is the fruit of that knowledge. For as love is the union of the Father and the Son, so is it also of God and the soul.

15. Hence it is that notwithstanding the most profound knowledge of God, and contemplation itself, together with the knowledge of all mysteries, the soul without love is worth nothing, and can do nothing, as the Apostle says, towards its union with God. [129] In another place he says, "Have charity, which is the bond of perfection." [130] This charity then and love of the soul make the Bridegroom run to drink of the fountain of the Bride's love, as the cooling waters attract the thirsty and the wounded hart, to be refreshed therein.

"And is refreshed."

16. As the air cools and refreshes him who is wearied with the heat, so the air of love refreshes and comforts him who burns with the fire of love. The fire of love has this property, the air which cools and refreshes it is an increase of the fire itself. To him who loves, love is a flame that burns with the desire of burning more and more, like the flame of material fire. The consummation of this desire of burning more and more, with the love of the bride, which is the air of her flight, is here called refreshment. The Bridegroom says in substance, "I burn more and more because of the ardor of your flight, for love kindles love."

17. God does not establish His grace and love in the soul but in proportion to the good will of that soul's love. He, therefore, that truly loves God must strive that his love fail not; for so, if we may thus speak, will he move God to show him greater love, and to take greater delight in his soul. In order to attain to such a degree of love, he must practice those things of which the Apostle speaks, saying: "Charity is patient, is benign: charity envies not, deals not perversely; is not puffed up, is not ambitious, seeks not her own, is not provoked to anger, thinks not evil, rejoices not upon iniquity, but rejoices with the truth; bears all things, believes all things, hopes all things, endures all things." [131]

NOTE

WHEN the dove -- that is the soul -- was flying on the gale of love over the waters of the deluge of the weariness and longing of its love, "not finding where her foot might rest," [132] the compassionate father Noah, in this last flight, put forth the hand of his mercy, caught her, and brought her into the ark of his charity and love. That took place when the Bridegroom, as in the stanza now explained, said, "Return, My Dove." In the shelter within the ark, the soul, finding all it desired, and more than it can ever express, begins to sing the praises of the Beloved, celebrating the magnificence which it feels and enjoys in that union, saying:

Footnotes:

123. See St. Teresa, Life,' ch. 20 sect. 16, or Las Mordadas,' 6. ch. 11.
124. Sect. 1. above.
125. Sect. 4. above.
126. 2 Cor. 12:3
127. See Relation' 8.
128. Sect. 1.
129. 1 Cor. 13:2
130. Col. 3:14
131. 1 Cor. 13:4-7
132. Gen. 8:9

A Spiritual Canticle of the Soul and the Bridegroom Christ

STANZAS XIV, XV

THE BRIDE

> My Beloved is the mountains,
> The solitary wooded valleys,
> The strange islands,
> The roaring torrents,
> The whisper of the amorous gales;
> The tranquil night
> At the approaches of the dawn,
> The silent music,
> The murmuring solitude,
> The supper which revives, and enkindles love.

BEFORE I begin to explain these stanzas, I must observe, in order that they and those which follow may be better understood, that this spiritual flight signifies a certain high estate and union of love, to which, after many spiritual exercises, God is wont to elevate the soul: it is called the spiritual betrothal of the Word, the Son of God. In the beginning, when this occurs the first time, God reveals to it great things of Himself, makes it beautiful in majesty and grandeur, adorns it with graces and gifts, and endows it with honor, and with the knowledge of Himself, as a bride is adorned on the day of her betrothal. On this happy day the soul not only ceases from its anxieties and loving complaints, but is, moreover, adorned with all grace, entering into a state of peace and delight, and of the sweetness of love, as it appears from these stanzas, in which it does nothing else but recount and praise the magnificence of the Beloved, which it recognizes in Him, and enjoys in the union of the betrothal.

2. In the stanzas that follow, the soul speaks no more of its anxieties and sufferings, as before, but of the sweet and peaceful intercourse of love with the Beloved; for now all its troubles are over. These two stanzas, which I am about to explain, contain all that God is wont at this time to bestow upon the soul; but we are not to suppose that all souls, thus far advanced, receive all that is here described, either in the same way or in the same degree of knowledge and of consciousness. Some souls receive more, others less; some in one way, some in another; and yet all may be in the state of spiritual betrothal. But in this stanza the highest possible is spoken of, because that embraces all.

EXPLANATION

3. As in the ark of Noah there were many chambers for the different kinds of animals, as the Sacred Writings tell us, and "all food that may be eaten," [133] so the soul, in its flight to the divine ark of the bosom of God, sees therein not only the many mansions of which our Lord speaks, but also all the food, that is, all the magnificence in which the soul may rejoice, and which are here referred to by the common terms of these stanzas. These are substantially as follows:

4. In this divine union the soul has a vision and foretaste of abundant and inestimable riches, and finds there all the repose and refreshment it desired; it attains to the secrets of God, and to a strange knowledge of Him, which is the food of those who know Him most; it is conscious of the awful power of God beyond all other power and might, tastes of the wonderful sweetness and delight of the Spirit, finds its true rest and divine light, drinks deeply of the wisdom of God, which shines forth in the harmony of the creatures and works of God; it feels itself filled with all good, emptied, and delivered from all evil, and, above all, rejoices consciously in the inestimable banquet of love which confirms it in love. This is the substance of these two stanzas.

5. The bride here says that her Beloved in Himself and to her is all the objects she enumerates; for in the ecstatic communications of God the soul feels and understands the truth of the saying of St. Francis: "God is mine and all things are mine." And because God is all, and the soul, and the good of all, the communication in this ecstasy is explained by the consideration that the goodness of the creatures referred to in these stanzas is a reflection of His goodness, as will appear from every line

thereof. All that is here set forth is in God eminently in an infinite way, or rather, every one of these grandeurs is God, and all of them together are God. Inasmuch as the soul is one with God, it feels all things to be God according to the words of St. John: "What was made, in Him was life." [134]

6. But we are not to understand this consciousness of the soul as if it saw the creatures in God as we see material objects in the light, but that it feels all things to be God in this fruition of Him; neither are we to imagine that the soul sees God essentially and clearly because it has so deep a sense of Him; for this is only a strong and abundant communication from Him, a glimmering light of what He is in Himself, by which the soul discerns this goodness of all things, as I proceed to explain.

"My Beloved is the mountains."

7. Mountains are high fertile, extensive, beautiful, lovely, flowery, and odorous. These mountains my Beloved is to me.

"The solitary wooded valleys."

8. Solitary valleys are tranquil, pleasant, cooling, shady, abounding in sweet waters, and by the variety of trees growing in them, and by the melody of the birds that frequent them, enliven and delight the senses; their solitude and silence procure us a refreshing rest. These valleys my Beloved is to me.

"The strange islands."

9. Strange islands are girt by the sea; they are also, because of the sea, distant and unknown to the commerce of men. They produce things very different from those with which we are conversant, in strange ways, and with qualities hitherto unknown, so as to surprise those who behold them, and fill them with wonder. Thus, then, by reason of the great and marvelous wonders, and the strange things that come to our knowledge, far beyond the common notions of men, which the soul beholds in God, it calls Him the strange islands. We say of a man that he is strange for one of two reasons: either because he withdraws himself from the society of his fellows, or because he is singular or distinguished in his life and conduct. For these two reasons together God is called strange by the soul. He is not only all that is strange in undiscovered islands, but His ways, judgments, and works are also strange, new, and marvelous to men.

10. It is nothing wonderful that God should be strange to men who have never seen Him, seeing that He is also strange to the holy angels and the souls who see Him; for they neither can nor shall ever see Him perfectly. Yes, even to the day of the last judgment they will see in Him so much that is new in His deep judgments, in His acts of mercy and justice, as to excite their wonder more and more. Thus God is the strange islands not to men only, but to the angels also; only to Himself is He neither strange nor new.

"The roaring torrents."

11. Torrents have three properties. 1. They overflow all that is in their course. 2. They fill all hollows. 3. They overpower all other sounds by their own. And hence the soul, feeling most sweetly that these three properties belong to God, says, "My Beloved is the roaring torrents."

12. As to the first property of which the soul is conscious, it feels itself to be so overwhelmed with the torrent of the Spirit of God, and so violently overpowered by it, that all the waters in the world seem to it to have surrounded it, and to have drowned all its former actions and passions. Though all this is violent, yet there is nothing painful in it, for these rivers are rivers of peace, as it is written, God, speaking through Isaiah, saying, "I will decline upon her, as it were, a flood of peace, and as a torrent overflowing glory." [135] That is, "I will bring upon the soul, as it were, a river of peace, and a torrent overflowing with glory." Thus this divine overflowing, like roaring torrents, fills the soul with peace and glory. The second property the soul feels is that this divine water is now filling the vessels of its humility and the emptiness of its desires, as it is written: "He has exalted the humble, and filled the hungry with good." [136] The third property of which the soul is now conscious in the roaring torrents of the Beloved is a spiritual sound and voice overpowering all other sounds and voices in the world. The explanation of this will take a little time.

13. This voice, or this murmuring sound of the waters, is an overflowing so abundant as to fill the soul with good, and a power so mighty seizing upon it as to seem not only the sound of many waters, but a most loud roaring of thunder. But the voice is a spiritual voice, unattended by material sounds or the pain and torment of them, but rather with majesty, power, might, delight, and glory: it is, as it were, a voice, an infinite interior sound which endows the soul with power and might. The Apostles heard in spirit this voice when the Holy Spirit descended upon them in the sound "as of a mighty wind," [137] as we

A Spiritual Canticle of the Soul and the Bridegroom Christ

read in the Acts of the Apostles. In order to manifest this spiritual voice, interiorly spoken, the sound was heard exteriorly, as of a rushing wind, by all those who were in Jerusalem. This exterior manifestation reveals what the Apostles interiorly received, namely, fullness of power and might.

14. So also when our Lord Jesus prayed to the Father because of His distress and the rage of His enemies, He heard an interior voice from heaven, comforting Him in His Sacred Humanity. The sound, solemn and grave, was heard exteriorly by the Jews, some of whom said that it thundered: others said, "An angel has spoken to Him." [138] The voice outwardly heard was the outward sign and expression of that strength and power which Christ then inwardly received in His human nature. We are not to suppose that the soul does not hear in spirit the spiritual voice because it is also outwardly heard. The spiritual voice is the effect on the soul of the audible voice, as material sounds strike the ear, and impress the meaning of it on the mind. This we learn from David when he said, "He will give to His voice the voice of strength;" [139] this strength is the interior voice. He will give to His voice -- that is, the outward voice, audibly heard -- the voice of strength which is felt within. God is an infinite voice, and communicating Himself thus to the soul produces the effect of an infinite voice.

15. This voice was heard by St. John, saying in the Revelation, "I heard a voice from heaven as the voice of many waters, and as the voice of great thunder." And, lest it should be supposed that a voice so strong was distressing and harsh, he adds immediately, "The voice which I heard was as the voice of harpers harping on their harps." [140] Ezekiel says that this sound as of many waters was "as it were the sound of the High God," [141] profoundly and sweetly communicated in it. This voice is infinite, because, as I have said, it is God Who communicates Himself, speaking in the soul; but He adapts Himself to each soul, uttering the voice of strength according to its capacity, in majesty and joy. And so the bride sings in the Canticle: "Let Your voice sound in my ears, for Your voice is sweet." [142]

"The whisper of the amorous gales."

16. Two things are to be considered here -- gales and whisper. The amorous gales are the virtues and graces of the Beloved, which, because of its union with the Bridegroom, play around the soul, and, most lovingly sent forth, touch it in their own substance. The whisper of the gales is a most sublime and sweet knowledge of God and of His attributes, which overflows into the understanding from the contact of the attributes of God with the substance of the soul. This is the highest delight of which the soul is capable in this life.

17. That we may understand this the better, we must keep in mind that as in a gale two things are observable -- the touch of it, and the whisper or sound -- so there are two things observable also in the communications of the Bridegroom -- the sense of delight, and the understanding of it. As the touch of the air is felt in the sense of touch, and the whisper of it heard in the ear, so also the contact of the perfections of the Beloved is felt and enjoyed in the touch of the soul -- that is, in the substance thereof, through the instrumentality of the will; and the knowledge of the attributes of God felt in the hearing of the soul -- that is, in the understanding.

18. The gale is said to blow amorously when it strikes deliciously, satisfying his desire who is longing for the refreshing which it ministers; for it then revives and soothes the sense of touch, and while the sense of touch is thus soothed, that of hearing also rejoices and delights in the sound and whisper of the gale more than the touch in the contact of the air, because the sense of hearing is more spiritual, or, to speak with greater correctness, is more nearly connected with the spiritual than is that of touch, and the delight thereof is more spiritual than is that of the touch. So also, inasmuch as this touch of God greatly satisfies and comforts the substance of the soul, sweetly fulfilling its longing to be received into union; this union, or touch, is called amorous gales, because, as I said before, the perfections of the Beloved are by it communicated to the soul lovingly and sweetly, and through it the whisper of knowledge to the understanding. It is called whisper, because, as the whisper of the air penetrates subtly into the organ of hearing, so this most subtle and delicate knowledge enters with marvelous sweetness and delight into the inmost substance of the soul, which is the highest of all delights.

19. The reason is that substantial knowledge is now communicated intelligibly, and stripped of all accidents and images, to the understanding, which philosophers call passive or passible, because inactive without any natural efforts of its own during this communication. This is the highest delight of the soul, because it is in the understanding, which is the seat of fruition, as theologians teach, and fruition is the vision of God. Some theologians think, inasmuch as this whisper signifies the substantial intelligence, that our father Elijah had a vision of God in the delicate whisper of the air, which he heard on the mount at the mouth of the cave. The Holy Scripture calls it "the whistling of a gentle wind," [143] because knowledge is begotten in the understanding by the subtle and delicate communication of the Spirit. The soul calls it here the whisper of the amorous gales, because it flows into the understanding from the loving communication of the perfections of the Beloved. This is why it is called the whisper of the amorous gales.

20. This divine whisper which enters in by the ear of the soul is not only substantial knowledge, but a manifestation also of the truths of the Divinity, and a revelation of the secret mysteries thereof. For in general, in the Holy Scriptures, every communication of God said to enter in by the ear is a manifestation of pure truths to the understanding, or a revelation of the secrets of God. These are revelations on purely spiritual visions, and are communicated directly to the soul without the intervention of the senses, and thus, what God communicates through the spiritual ear is most profound and most certain. When St. Paul would express the greatness of the revelations made to him, he did not say, "I saw or I perceived secret words," but "I heard secret words which it is not granted to man to utter." [144] It is thought that St. Paul also saw God, as our father Elijah, in the whisper of a gentle air. For as "faith comes by hearing" -- so the Apostle teaches -- that is, by the hearing of the material ear, so also that which the faith teaches, the intelligible truth, comes by spiritual hearing.

21. The prophet Job, speaking to God, when He revealed Himself to him, teaches the same doctrine, saying, "With the hearing of the ear I have heard You, but now my eye sees You." [145] It is clear, from this, that to hear with the ear of the soul is to see with the eye of the passive understanding. He does not say, "I heard with the hearing of my ears," but "with the hearing of my ear"; nor, "with the seeing of my eyes," but "with the eye of my understanding"; the hearing of the soul is, therefore, the vision of the understanding.

22. Still, we are not to think that what the soul perceives, though pure truth, can be the perfect and clear fruition of Heaven. For though it is free from accidents, as I said before, [146] it is dim and not clear, because it is contemplation, which in this life, as St. Dionysius says, "is a ray of darkness," [147] and thus we may say that it is a ray and an image of fruition, because it is in the understanding, which is the seat of fruition. This substantial truth, called here a whisper, is the "eyes desired" which the Beloved showed to the bride, who, unable to bear the vision, cried, "Turn them away, O my Beloved." [148]

23. There is a passage in the book of Job which greatly confirms what I have said of rapture and betrothal, and, because I consider it to be much to the purpose, I will give it here, though it may delay us a little, and explain those portions of it which belong to my subject. The explanation shall be short, and when I shall have made it, I shall go on to explain the other stanza. The passage is as follows: "To me there was spoken a secret word," said Eliphaz the Themanite, "and, as it were, my ear by stealth received the veins of its whisper. In the horror of a vision by night, when deep sleep is wont to hold men, fear held me and trembling, and all my bones were made sore afraid: and when the spirit passed before me the hair of my flesh stood upright. There stood one whose countenance I knew not, an image before my eyes, and I heard the voice, as it were, of a gentle wind." [149]

24. This passage contains almost all I said about rapture in the thirteenth stanza, where the bride says: "Turn them away, O my Beloved." The "word spoken in secret" to Eliphaz is that secret communication which by reason of its greatness the soul was not able to endure, and, therefore, cried out: "Turn them away, O my Beloved." Eliphaz says that his "ear as it were by stealth received the veins of its whisper." By that is meant the pure substance which the understanding receives, for the "veins" here denote the interior substance. The whisper is that communication and touch of the virtues whereby the said substance is communicated to the understanding. It is called a whisper because of its great gentleness. And the soul calls it the amorous gales because it is lovingly communicated. It is said to be received as it were by stealth, for as that which is stolen is alienated, so this secret is alien to man, speaking in the order of nature, because that which he received does not appertain to him naturally, and thus it was not lawful for him to receive it; neither was it lawful for St. Paul to repeat what he heard. For this reason the prophet says twice, "My secret to myself, my secret to myself." [150]

25. When Eliphaz speaks of the horror of the vision by night, and of the fear and trembling that seized upon him, he refers to the awe and dread that comes upon the soul naturally in rapture, because in its natural strength it is unable, as I said before, [151] to endure the communication of the Spirit of God. The prophet gives us to understand that, as when sleep is about to fall upon men, a certain vision which they call a nightmare is wont to oppress and terrify them in the interval between sleeping and waking, which is the moment of the approach of sleep, so in the spiritual passage between the sleep of natural ignorance and the waking of the supernatural understanding, which is the beginning of an ecstasy or rapture, the spiritual vision then revealed makes the soul fear and tremble.

26. "All my bones were affrighted"; that is, were shaken and disturbed. By this he meant a certain dislocation of the bones which takes place when the soul falls into an ecstasy. This is clearly expressed by Daniel when he saw the angel, saying, "O my lord, at the sight of you my joints are loosed." [152] "When the spirit passed before me" -- that is, "When my spirit was made to transcend the ways and limitations of nature in ecstasies and raptures" -- "the hair of my flesh stood upright"; that is, "my body was chilled, and the flesh contracted, like that of a dead man."

27. "There stood One" -- that is God, Who reveals Himself after this manner -- "Whose countenance knew not": in these communications or visions, however high they may be, the soul neither knows nor beholds the face and being of God. "An image before my eyes"; that is, the knowledge of the secret words was most deep, as it were the image and face of God; but still this is not the essential

A Spiritual Canticle of the Soul and the Bridegroom Christ

vision of God. "I heard the voice, as it were, of a gentle wind"; this is the whisper of the amorous gales -- that is, of the Beloved of the soul.

28. But it is not to be supposed that these visits of God are always attended by such terrors and distress of nature: that happens to them only who are entering the state of illumination and perfection, and in this kind of communication; for in others they come with great sweetness.

Footnotes:

133. Gen. 6:21
134. John 1:3, 4. See Stanza viii.
135. Isa. 66:12
136. Luke 1:52
137. Acts 2:2
138. John 12:29
139. Ps. 67:34
140. Rev. 14:2
141. Ezek. 1:24
142. Cant. 2:14
143. 1 Kings 19:12
144. 2 Cor. 12:4
145. Job 42:5
146. Sect. 20.
147. De Mystica Theologia,' ch. i.
148. Cant. 6:4
149. Job 4:12-16
150. Isa. 24:16
151. Stan. xiii. sect. 1.
152. Dan. 10:16

St. John of the Cross

STANZA XV

"THE tranquil night." In this spiritual sleep in the bosom of the Beloved the soul is in possession and fruition of all the calm, repose, and quiet of a peaceful night, and receives at the same time in God a certain dim, unfathomable divine intelligence. This is the reason why it says that the Beloved is to it the tranquil night.

2. "At the approaches of the dawn." This tranquil night is not like a night of darkness, but rather like the night when the sunrise is drawing nigh. This tranquillity and repose in God is not all darkness to the soul, as the dark night is, but rather tranquillity and repose in the divine light and in a new knowledge of God, whereby the mind, most sweetly tranquil, is raised to a divine light.

3. This divine light is here very appropriately called the approaches of the dawn, that is, the twilight; for as the twilight of the morn disperses the darkness of the night and reveals the light of day, so the mind, tranquil and reposing in God, is raised up from the darkness of natural knowledge to the morning light of the supernatural knowledge of God; not clear, indeed, as I have said, but dim, like the night at the approaches of the dawn. For as it is then neither wholly night nor wholly day, but, as they say, twilight, so this solitude and divine repose is neither perfectly illumined by the divine light nor yet perfectly alien from it.

4. In this tranquillity the understanding is lifted up in a strange way above its natural comprehension to the divine light: it is like a man who, after a profound sleep, opens his eyes to unexpected light. This knowledge is referred to by David when he says, "I have watched, and am become as the lonely sparrow on the housetop"; [153] that is, "I opened the eyes of my understanding and was raised up above all natural comprehension, lonely, without them, on the housetop, lifted up above all earthly considerations." He says that he was "become as the lonely sparrow," because in this kind of contemplation, the spirit has the properties of the sparrow. These are five in number:

i. It frequents in general high places; and the spirit, in this state, rises to the highest contemplation.

ii. It is ever turning its face in the direction of the wind, and thespirit turns its affections thither whence comes the spirit of love, which is God.

iii. It is in general solitary, abstaining from the companionship of others, and flying away when any approach it: so the spirit, in contemplation, is far away from all worldly thoughts, lonely in its avoidance of them; neither does it consent to anything except to this solitude in God.

iv. It sings most sweetly, and so also does the spirit at this time sing to God; for the praises which it offers up proceed from the sweetest love, most pleasing to itself, and most precious in the sight of God.

v. It is of no definite color; so also is the perfect spirit, which in this ecstasy is not only without any tinge of sensual affection or self-love, but also without any particular consideration of the things of heaven or earth; neither can it give any account whatever of them, because it has entered into the abyss of the knowledge of God.

"The silent music."

5. In this silence and tranquillity of the night, and in this knowledge of the divine light, the soul discerns a marvelous arrangement and disposition of God's wisdom in the diversities of His creatures and operations. All these, and each one of them, have a certain correspondence with God, whereby each, by a voice peculiar to itself, proclaims what there is in itself of God, so as to form a concert of sublimest melody, transcending all the harmonies of the world. This is the silent music, because it is knowledge tranquil and calm, without audible voice; and thus the sweetness of music and the repose of silence are enjoyed in it. The soul says that the Beloved is silent music, because this harmony of spiritual music is in Him understood and felt. He is not this only, He is also --

"The murmuring solitude."

6. This is almost the same as the silent music. For though the music is inaudible to the senses and the natural powers, it is a solitude most full of sound to the spiritual powers. These powers being in solitude, emptied of all forms and natural apprehensions, may well receive in spirit, like a resounding

A Spiritual Canticle of the Soul and the Bridegroom Christ

voice, the spiritual impression of the majesty of God in Himself and in His creatures; as it happened to St. John, who heard in spirit as it were "the voice of harpers harping on their harps." [154] St. John heard this in spirit: it was not material harps that he heard, but a certain knowledge that he had of the praises of the blessed, which every one of them, each in his own degree of glory, is continually singing before God. It is as it were music. For as every one of the saints had the gifts of God in a different way, so every one of them sings His praises in a different way, and yet all harmonize in one concert of love, as in music.

7. In the same way, in this tranquil contemplation, the soul beholds all creatures, not only the highest, but the lowest also, each one according to the gift of God to it, sending forth the voice of its witness to what God is. It beholds each one magnifying Him in its own way, and possessing Him according to its particular capacity; and thus all these voices together unite in one strain in praise of God's greatness, wisdom, and marvelous knowledge. This is the meaning of those words of the Holy Spirit in the Book of Wisdom: "The Spirit of our Lord has replenished the whole world, and that which contains all things has the knowledge of the voice." [155] "The voice" is the murmuring solitude, which the soul is said to know, namely, the witness which all things bear to God. Inasmuch as the soul hears this music only in solitude and in estrangement from all outward things, it calls it silent music and murmuring solitude. These are the Beloved.

"The supper which revives, and enkindles love."

8. Lovers find recreation, satisfaction, and love in feasts. And because the Beloved in this sweet communication produces these three effects in the soul, He is here said to be the supper that revives, and enkindles love. In Holy Scripture supper signifies the divine vision, for as supper is the conclusion of the day's labors, and the beginning of the night's repose, so the soul in this tranquil knowledge is made to feel that its trials are over, the possession of good begun, and its love of God increased. Hence, then, the Beloved is to the soul the supper that revives, in being the end of its trials, and that enkindles love, in being the beginning of the fruition of all good.

9. That we may see more clearly how the Bridegroom is the supper of the soul, we must refer to those words of the Beloved in the Revelation: "Behold, I stand at the door and knock. If any man shall hear My voice, and open to Me the gate, I will enter into him, and will sup with him, and he with Me."[156] It is evident from these words that He brings the supper with Him, which is nothing else but His own sweetness and delights, wherein He rejoices Himself, and which He, uniting Himself to the soul, communicates to it, making it a partaker of His joy: for this is the meaning of "I will sup with him, and he with Me." These words describe the effect of the divine union of the soul with God, wherein it shares the very goods of God Himself, Who communicates them graciously and abundantly to it. Thus the Beloved is Himself the supper which revives, and enkindles love, refreshing the soul with His abundance, and enkindling its love in His graciousness.

10. But before I proceed to explain the stanzas which follow, I must observe that, in the state of betrothal, wherein the soul enjoys this tranquillity, and wherein it receives all that it can receive in this life, we are not to suppose its tranquillity to be perfect, but that the higher part of it is tranquil; for the sensual part, except in the state of spiritual marriage, never loses all its imperfect habits, and its powers are never wholly subdued, as I shall show hereafter. [157] What the soul receives now is all that it can receive in the state of betrothal, for in that of the marriage the blessings are greater. Though the bride-soul has great joy in these visits of the Beloved in the state of betrothal, still it has to suffer from His absence, to endure trouble and afflictions in the lower part, and at the hands of the devil. But all this ceases in the state of spiritual marriage.

NOTE

THE bride now in possession of the virtues in their perfection, whereby she is ordinarily rejoicing in peace when the Beloved visits her, is now and then in the fruition of the fragrance and sweetness of those virtues in the highest degree, because the Beloved touches them within her, just as the sweetness and beauty of the lilies and other flowers when in their bloom are perceived when we handle them. For in many of these visits the soul discerns within itself all its virtues which God has given it; He shedding light upon them. The soul now, with marvelous joy and sweetness of love, binds them together and presents them to the Beloved as a nosegay of beautiful flowers, and the Beloved in accepting them -- for He truly accepts them then -- accepts thereby a great service. All this takes place within the soul, feeling that the Beloved is within it as on His own couch, for the soul presents itself with the virtues which is the greatest service it can render Him, and thus this is one of the greatest joys which in its interior conversation with God the soul is wont to receive in presents of this kind made to the Beloved.

2. The devil, beholding this prosperity of the soul, and in his great malice envying all the good he

sees in it, now uses all his power, and has recourse to all his devices, in order to thwart it, if possible, even in the slightest degree. He thinks it of more consequence to keep back the soul, even for an instant, from this abundance, bliss, and delight, than to make others fall into many and mortal sins. Other souls have little or nothing to lose, while this soul has much, having gained many and great treasures; for the loss of one grain of refined gold is greater than the loss of many of the baser metals.

3. The devil here has recourse to the sensual appetites, though now they can give him generally but little or no help because they are mortified, and because he cannot turn them to any great account in distracting the imagination. Sometimes he stirs up many movements in the sensitive part of the soul, and causes other vexations, spiritual as well as sensual, from which the soul is unable to deliver itself until our Lord shall send His angel, as it is written, "The angel of the Lord shall put in himself about them that fear Him, and shall deliver them;" [158] and so establish peace, both in the spiritual and sensitive parts of the soul. With a view to show forth this truth, and to ask this favor, the soul, apprehensive by experience of the craft which the devil makes use of to thwart this good, addressing itself to the angels, whose function it is to succor it at this time by putting the evil spirits to flight, speaks as in the following stanza:

Footnotes:

153. Ps. 101:8
154. Rev. 14:2
155. Wisd. 1:7
156. Rev. 3:20
157. Stanza xxvi.
158. Ps. 33:8

STANZA XVI

Catch us the foxes,
For our vineyard has flourished;
While of roses
We make a nosegay,
And let no one appear on the hill.

THE soul, anxious that this interior delight of love, which is the flowers of the vineyard, should not be interrupted, either by envious and malicious devils, or the raging desires of sensuality, or the various comings and goings of the imagination, or any other consciousness or presence of created things, calls upon the angels to seize and hinder all these from interrupting its practice of interior love, in the joy and sweetness of which the soul and the Son of God communicate and delight in the virtues and graces.

"Catch us the foxes, for our vineyard has flourished."

2. The vineyard is the plantation in this holy soul of all the virtues which minister to it the wine of sweet taste. The vineyard of the soul is then flourishing when it is united in will to the Bridegroom, and delights itself in Him in all the virtues. Sometimes, as I have just said, the memory and the fancy are assailed by various forms and imaginings, and diverse motions and desires trouble the sensual part. The great variety and diversity of these made David say, when he felt the inconvenience and the trouble of them as he was drinking of the sweet wine of the spirit, thirsting greatly after God: "For You my soul has thirsted, for You my flesh, O how many ways." [159]

3. Here the soul calls the whole troop of desires and stirrings of sense, foxes, because of the great resemblance between them at this time. As foxes pretend to be asleep that they may pounce upon their prey when it comes in their way, so all the desires and powers of sense in the soul are asleep until the flowers of virtue grow, flourish, and bloom. Then the desires and powers of sense awake to resist the Spirit and domineer. "The flesh lusts against the spirit," [160] and as the inclination of it is towards the sensual desires, it is disgusted as soon as it tastes of the Spirit, and herein the desires prove extremely troublesome to spiritual sweetness.

"Catch us the foxes."

. The evil spirits now molest the soul in two ways. They vehemently excite the desires, and employ them with other imaginations to assail the peaceful and flourishing kingdom of the soul. Then -- and this is much worse -- when they do not succeed in stirring up the desires, they assail the soul with bodily pains and noises in order to distract it. And, what is still more serious, they fight with spiritual horror and dread, and sometimes with fearful torments, which, at this time, if God permits them, they can most effectually bring about, for inasmuch as the soul is now spiritually detached, so as to perform its spiritual exercises, the devil being himself a spirit presents himself before it with great ease.

5. At other times the evil spirit assails the soul with other horrors, before it begins to have the fruition of the sweet flowers, when God is beginning to draw it forth out of the house of sense that it may enter on the interior exercises in the garden of the Bridegroom, for he knows well that once entered into this state of recollection it is there so protected that, notwithstanding all he can do, he cannot hurt it. Very often, too, when the devil goes forth to meet the soul, the soul becomes quickly recollected in the secret depths of its interior, where it finds great sweetness and protection; then those terrors of Satan are so far off that they not only produce no fear, but are even the occasion of peace and joy. The bride, in the Canticle, speaks of these terrors, saying, "My soul troubled me for the chariots of Aminadab." [161] Aminadab is the evil spirit, and his chariots are his assaults upon the soul, which he makes with great violence, noise, and confusion.

6. The bride also says what the soul says here, namely: "Catch us the little foxes that destroy the vineyards; for our vineyard has flourished." [162] She does not say, "Catch me" but "Catch us," because she is speaking of herself and the Beloved; for they are one, and enjoy the flourishing of the vineyard

together.

7. The reason why the vineyard is said to be flourishing and not bearing fruit is this: the soul in this life has the fruition of virtues, however perfect they may be, only in their flower, because the fruit of them is reserved for the life to come.

"While of roses we make a nosegay."

8. Now, at this time, while the soul is rejoicing in the flourishing of the vineyard, and delighting itself in the bosom of the Beloved, all its virtues are perfect, exhibiting themselves to the soul, and sending forth great sweetness and delight. The soul feels them to be in itself and in God so as to seem to be one vineyard most flourishing and pleasing belonging to both, wherein they feed and delight. Then the soul binds all its virtues together, makes acts of love in each of them separately, and in all together, and then offers them all to the Beloved, with great tenderness of love and sweetness, and in this the Beloved helps it, for without His help and favor it cannot make this union and oblation of virtue to the Beloved. Hence it says, "We make a nosegay" -- that is "the Beloved and myself."

9. This union of the virtues is called a nosegay; for as a nosegay is cone-like in form, and a cone is strong, containing and embracing many pieces firmly joined together, so this cone-like nosegay of the virtues which the soul makes for the Beloved is the uniform perfection of the soul which firmly and solidly contains and embraces many perfections, great virtues, and rich endowments; for all the perfections and virtues of the soul unite together to form but one. And while this perfection is being accomplished, and when accomplished, offered to the Beloved on the part of the soul, it becomes necessary to catch the foxes that they may not hinder this mutual interior communication. The soul prays not only that this nosegay may be carefully made, but also adds, "And let no one appear on the hill."

10. This divine interior exercise requires solitude and detachment from all things, whether in the lower part of the soul, which is that of sense, or in the higher, which is the rational. These two divisions comprise all the faculties and senses of man, and are here called the hill; because all our natural notions and desires being in them, as quarry on a hill, the devil lies in wait among these notions and desires, in order that he may injure the soul.

"And let no one appear on the hill."

11. That is, let no representation or image of any object whatever, appertaining to any of these faculties or senses, appear in the presence of the soul and the Bridegroom: in other words, let the spiritual powers of the soul, memory, understanding, and will, be divested of all notions, particular inclinations, or considerations whatsoever; and let all the senses and faculties of the body, interior as well as exterior, the imagination, the fancy, the sight and hearing, and the rest, be divested of all occasions of distractions, of all forms, images, and representations, and of all other natural operations.

12. The soul speaks in this way because it is necessary for the perfect fruition of this communication of God, that all the senses and powers, both interior and exterior, should be disencumbered and emptied of their proper objects and operations; for the more active they are, the greater will be the hindrance which they will occasion. The soul having attained to a certain interior union of love, the spiritual faculties of it are no longer active, and still less those of the body; for now that the union of love is actually wrought in love, the faculties of the soul cease from their exertions, because now that the goal is reached all employment of means is at an end. What the soul at this time has to do is to wait lovingly upon God, and this waiting is love in a continuation of unitive love. Let no one, therefore, appear on the hill, but the will only waiting on the Beloved in the offering up of self and of all the virtues in the way described.

NOTE

FOR the clearer understanding of the following stanza, we must keep in mind that the absence of the Beloved, from which the soul suffers in the state of spiritual betrothal, is an exceedingly great affliction, and at times greater than all other trials whatever. The reason is this: the love of the soul for God is now so vehement and deep that the pain of His absence is vehement and deep also. This pain is increased also by the annoyance which comes from intercourse with creatures, which is very great; for the soul, under the pressure of its quickened desire of union with God, finds all other conversation most painful and difficult to endure. It is like a stone in its flight to the place whither it is rapidly tending; every obstacle it meets with occasions a violent shock. And as the soul has tasted of the sweetness of the Beloved's visits, which are more desirable than gold and all that is beautiful, it therefore dreads even a momentary absence, and addresses itself as follows to aridities, and to the Spirit of the Bridegroom: --

A Spiritual Canticle of the Soul and the Bridegroom Christ
Footnotes:
159. Ps. 62:2
160. Gal. 5:17
161. Cant. 6:11
162. Cant. 2:15

STANZA XVII

O killing north wind, cease!
Come, south wind, that awakens love!
Blow through my garden,
And let its odors flow,
And the Beloved shall feed among the flowers.

BESIDE the causes mentioned in the foregoing stanza, spiritual dryness also hinders the fruition of this interior sweetness of which I have been speaking, and afraid of it the soul had recourse to two expedients, to which it refers in the present stanza. The first is to shut the door against it by unceasing prayer and devotion. The second, to invoke the Holy Spirit; it is He Who drives away dryness from the soul, maintains and increases its love of the Bridegroom -- that He may establish in it the practice of virtue, and all this to the end that the Son of God, its Bridegroom, may rejoice and delight in it more and more, for its only aim is to please the Beloved.

"Killing north wind, cease."

2. The north wind is exceedingly cold; it dries up and parches flowers and plants, and at the least, when it blows, causes them to draw in and shrink. So, dryness of spirit and the sensible absence of the Beloved, because they produce the same effect on the soul, exhausting the sweetness and fragrance of virtue, are here called the killing north wind; for all the virtues and affective devotions of the soul are then dead. Hence the soul addresses itself to it, saying, "Killing north wind, cease." These words mean that the soul applies itself to spiritual exercise, in order to escape aridity. But the communications of God are now so interior that by no exertion of its faculties can the soul attain to them if the Spirit of the Bridegroom do not cause these movements of love. The soul, therefore, addresses Him, saying:

"Come, south wind, that awakens love."

3. The south wind is another wind commonly called the south-west wind. It is soft, and brings rain; it makes the grass and plants grow, flowers to blossom and scatter their perfume abroad; in short, it is the very opposite in its effects of the north wind. By it is meant here the Holy Spirit, Who awakens love; for when this divine Breath breathes on the soul, it so inflames and refreshes it, so quickens the will, and stirs up the desires, which were before low and asleep as to the love of God, that we may well say of it that it quickens the love between Him and the soul. The prayer of the soul to the Holy Spirit is thus expressed, "Blow through my garden."

4. This garden is the soul itself. For as the soul said of itself before, that it was a flourishing vineyard, because the flowers of virtue which are in it give forth the wine of sweetness, so here it says of itself that it is a garden, because the flowers of perfection and the virtues are planted in it, flourish, and grow.

5. Observe, too, that the expression is "blow through my garden," not blow in it. There is a great difference between God's breathing into the soul and through it. To breathe into the soul is to infuse into it graces, gifts, and virtues; to breathe through it is, on the part of God, to touch and move its virtues and perfections now possessed, renewing them and stirring them in such a way that they send forth their marvelous fragrance and sweetness. Thus aromatic spices, when shaken or touched, give forth the abundant odors which are not otherwise so distinctly perceived. The soul is not always in the conscious fruition of its acquired and infused virtues, because, in this life, they are like flowers in seed, or in bud, or like aromatic spices covered over, the perfume of which is not perceived till they are exposed and shaken.

6. But God sometimes is so merciful to the bride-soul, as -- the Holy Spirit breathing meanwhile through the flourishing garden -- to open these buds of virtue and expose the aromatic herbs of the soul's gifts, perfections, and riches, to manifest to it its interior treasures and to reveal to it all its beauty. It is then marvelous to behold, and sweet to feel, the abundance of the gifts now revealed in the soul, and the beauty of the flowers of virtue now flourishing in it. No language can describe the fragrance which

A Spiritual Canticle of the Soul and the Bridegroom Christ

every one of them diffuses, each according to its kind. This state of the soul is referred to in the words, "Let its odors flow."

7. So abundant are these odors at times, that the soul seems enveloped in delight and bathed in inestimable bliss. Not only is it conscious itself of them, but they even overflow it, so that those who know how to discern these things can perceive them. The soul in this state seems to them as a delectable garden, full of the joys and riches of God. This is observable in holy souls, not only when the flowers open, but almost always; for they have a certain air of grandeur and dignity which inspires the beholders with awe and reverence, because of the supernatural effects of their close and familiar conversation with God. We have an illustration of this in the life of Moses, the sight of whose face the people could not bear, by reason of the glory that rested upon it -- the effect of his speaking to God face to face. [163]

8. While the Holy Spirit is breathing through the garden -- this is His visitation of the soul -- the Bridegroom Son of God communicates Himself to it in a profound way, enamored of it. It is for this that He sends the Holy Spirit before Him -- as He sent the Apostles [164] -- to make ready the chamber of the soul His bride, comforting it with delight, setting its garden in order, opening its flowers, revealing its gifts, and adorning it with the tapestry of graces. The bride-soul longs for this with all its might, and therefore bids the north wind not to blow, and invokes the south wind to blow through the garden, because she gains much here at once.

9. The bride now gains the fruition of all her virtues in their sweetest exercise. She gains the fruition of her Beloved in them, because it is through them that He converses with her in most intimate love, and grants her favors greater than any of the past. She gains, too, that her Beloved delights more in her because of the actual exercise of virtue, which is what pleases her most, namely, that her Beloved should be pleased with her. She gains also the permanent continuance of the sweet fragrance which remains in the soul while the Bridegroom is present, and the bride entertains Him with the sweetness of her virtues, as it is written: "While the King was at His repose," that is, in the soul, "my spikenard sent forth its odor." [165] The spikenard is the soul, which from the flowers of its virtues sends forth sweet odors to the Beloved, Who dwells within it in the union of love.

10. It is therefore very much to be desired that every soul should pray the Holy Spirit to blow through its garden, that the divine odors of God may flow. And as this is so necessary, so blissful and profitable to the soul, the bride desires it, and prays for it, in the words of the Canticle, saying, "Arise, north wind, and come, south wind; blow through my garden, and let the aromatic spices thereof flow."[166] The soul prays for this, not because of the delight and bliss consequent upon it, but because of the delight it ministers to the Beloved, and because it prepares the way and announces the presence of the Son of God, Who comes to rejoice in it. Hence the soul adds:

"And my Beloved shall feed among the flowers."

11. The delight which the Son of God finds now in the soul is described as pasture. This word expresses most forcibly the truth, because pasture not only gladdens, but also sustains. Thus the Son of God delights in the soul, in the delights thereof, and is sustained in them -- that is, He abides within it as in a place which pleases Him exceedingly, because the place itself really delights in Him. This, I believe, is the meaning of those words recorded in the proverbs of Solomon: "My delights were to be with the children of men;" [167] that is, when they delight to be with Me, Who am the Son of God.

12. Observe, here, that it is not said that the Beloved shall feed on the flowers, but that He shall feed among the flowers. For, as the communications of the Beloved are in the soul itself, through the adornment of the virtues, it follows that what He feeds on is the soul which He transformed into Himself, now that it is prepared and adorned with these flowers of virtues, graces, and perfections, which are the things whereby, and among which, He feeds. These, by the power of the Holy Spirit, are sending forth in the soul the odors of sweetness to the Son of God, that He may feed there the more in the love thereof; for this is the love of the Bridegroom, to be united to the soul amid the fragrance of the flowers.

13. The bride in the Canticle has observed this, for she had experience of it, saying: "My Beloved is gone down into His garden, to the bed of aromatic spices,

to feed in the gardens, and to gather lilies. I to my Beloved, and my Beloved to me, Who feeds among the lilies." [168] That is, "Who feeds and delights in my soul, which is His garden, among the lilies of my virtues, perfections, and graces."

NOTE

IN the state of spiritual espousals the soul contemplating its great riches and excellence, but unable to enter into the possession and fruition of them as it desires, because it is still in the flesh, often suffers exceedingly, and then more particularly when its knowledge of them becomes more profound. It then sees itself in the body, like a prince in prison, subject to all misery, whose authority is disregarded, whose territories and wealth are confiscated, and who of his former substance receives but a miserable dole. How greatly he suffers anyone may see, especially when his household is no longer obedient, and his slaves and servants, forgetting all respect, plunder him of the scanty provisions of his table. Thus is it with the soul in the body, for when God mercifully admits it to a foretaste of the good things which He has prepared for it, the wicked servants of desire in the sensual part, now a slave of disorderly motions, now other rebellious movements, rise up against it in order to rob it of its good.

2. The soul feels itself as if it were in the land of enemies, tyrannized over by the stranger, like the dead among the dead. Its feelings are those which the prophet Baruch gave vent to when he described the misery of Jacob's captivity: "How happens it, O Israel, that you are in your enemies' land? You have grown old in a strange country, you are defiled with the dead: you are counted with them that go down into hell." [169] This misery of the soul, in the captivity of the body, is thus spoken of by Jeremiah, saying: "Is Israel a bondman or a home-born slave? Why then is he become a prey? The lions have roared upon him, and have made a noise." [170] The lions are the desires and the rebellious motions of the tyrant king of sensuality. In order to express the trouble which this tyrant occasions, and the desire of the soul to see this kingdom of sensuality with all its hosts destroyed, or wholly subject to the spirit, the soul lifting up its eyes to the Bridegroom, as to one who can effect it, speaks against those rebellious motions in the words of the next stanza.

Footnotes:

163. Exod. 34:30
164. Luke 22:8
165. Cant. 1:11
166. Cant. 4:16
167. Prov. 8:31
168. Cant. 6:1, 2
169. Bar. 3:10, 11
170. Jer. 2:14, 15

A Spiritual Canticle of the Soul and the Bridegroom Christ

STANZA XVIII

O nymphs of Judea!
While amid the flowers and the rose-trees
The amber sends forth its perfume,
Tarry in the suburbs,
And touch not our thresholds.

IT is the bride that speaks; for seeing herself, as to the higher part of the soul, adorned with the rich endowments of her Beloved, and seeing Him delighting in her, she desires to preserve herself in security, and in the continued fruition of them. Seeing also that hindrances will arise, as in fact they do, from the sensual part of the soul, which will disturb so great a good, she bids the operations and motions of the soul's lower nature to cease, in the senses and faculties of it, and sensuality not to overstep its boundaries to trouble and disquiet the higher and spiritual portion of the soul: not to hinder even for a moment the sweetness she enjoys. The motions of the lower part, and their powers, if they show themselves during the enjoyment of the spirit, are so much more troublesome and disturbing, the more active they are.

"*O nymphs of Judea.*"

2. The lower, that is the sensual part of the soul, is called Judea. It is called Judea because it is weak, and carnal, and blind, like the Jewish people. All the imaginations, fancies, motions, and inclinations of the lower part of the soul are called nymphs, for as nymphs with their beauty and attractions entice men to love them, so the operations and motions of sensuality softly and earnestly strive to entice the will from the rational part, in order to withdraw it from that which is interior, and to fix it on that which is exterior, to which they are prone themselves. They also strive to influence the understanding to join with them in their low views, and to bring down reason to the level of sense by the attractions of the latter. The soul, therefore, says in effect: "O sensual operations and motions."

"*While amid the flowers and the rose-trees.*"

3. The flowers, as I have said, are the virtues of the soul, and the rose-trees are its powers, memory, understanding, and will, which produce and nurture the flowers of divine conceptions, acts of love and the virtues, while the amber sends forth its perfume in the virtues and powers of the soul.

"*The amber sends forth its perfume.*"

4. The amber is the divine spirit of the Bridegroom Who dwells in the soul. To send forth the perfume among the flowers and the rose-trees, is to diffuse and communicate Himself most sweetly in the powers and virtues of the soul, thereby filling it with the perfume of divine sweetness. Meanwhile, then, when the Divine Spirit is filling my soul with spiritual sweetness,

"*Tarry in the suburbs.*"

5. In the suburbs of Judea, which is the inferior or sensual part of the soul. The suburbs are the interior senses, namely, memory, fancy, and imagination, where forms and images of things collect, by the help of which sensuality stirs up concupiscence and desires. These forms are the nymphs, and while they are quiet and tranquil the desires are also asleep. They enter into the suburbs of the interior senses by the gates of the outward senses, of sight, hearing, smell, etc. We can thus give the name of suburbs to all the powers and interior or exterior senses of the sensual part of the soul, because they are outside the walls of the city.

6. That part of the soul which may be called the city is that which is most interior, the rational part, which is capable of conversation with God, the operations of which are contrary to those of sensuality. But there is a natural intercourse between those who dwell in the suburbs of the sensual part -- that is,

the nymphs -- and those who dwell in the higher part, which is the city itself; and, therefore, what takes place in the lower part is ordinarily felt in the higher, and consequently compels attention to itself and disturbs the spiritual operation which is conversant with God. Hence the soul bids the nymphs tarry in the suburbs -- that is, to remain at rest in the exterior and interior senses of the sensual part,

"And touch not our thresholds."

7. Let not even your first movements touch the higher part, for the first movements of the soul are the entrance and thresholds of it. When the first movements have passed into the reason, they have crossed the threshold, but when they remain as first movements only they are then said merely to touch the threshold, or to cry at the gate, which is the case when reason and sense contend over an unreasonable act. The soul here not only bids these not to touch it, but also charges all considerations whatever which do not minister to its repose and the good it enjoys to keep far away.

NOTE

THE soul in this state is become so great an enemy of the lower part, and its operations, that it would have God communicate nothing to it when He communicates with the higher. If He will communicate with the lower, it must be in a slight degree, or the soul, because of its natural weakness, will be unable to endure it without fainting, and consequently the spirit cannot rejoice in peace, because it is then troubled. "For," as the wise man says, "the body that is corrupted burdens the soul." [171] And as the soul longs for the highest and noblest conversation with God, which is impossible in the company of the sensual part, it begs of God to deal with it without the intervention of the senses. That sublime vision of St. Paul in the third heaven, wherein, he says, he saw God, but yet knew not whether he was in the body or out of the body, must have been, be it what it may, independent of the body: for if the body had any share in it, he must have known it, and the vision could not have been what it was, seeing that he "heard secret words which it is not lawful for a man to speak." [172] The soul, therefore, knowing well that graces so great cannot be received in a vessel so mean, and longing to receive them out of the body, -- or at least without it, addresses the Bridegroom in the words that follow:

Footnotes:

171. Wisd. 9:15
172. 2 Cor. 12:2-4

A Spiritual Canticle of the Soul and the Bridegroom Christ

STANZA XIX

Hide yourself, O my Beloved!
Turn Your face to the mountains,
Do not speak,
But regard the companions
Of her who is traveling amidst strange islands.

HERE the bride presents four petitions to the Bridegroom. She prays that He would be pleased to converse with her most interiorly in the secret chamber of the soul. The second, that He would invest and inform her faculties with the glory and excellence of His Divinity. The third, that He would converse with her so profoundly as to surpass all knowledge and expression, and in such a way that the exterior and sensual part may not perceive it. The fourth, that He would love the many virtues and graces which He has implanted in her, adorned with which she is ascending upwards to God in the highest knowledge of the Divinity, and in transports of love most strange and singular, surpassing those of ordinary experience.

"Hide Yourself, O my Beloved!"

2. "O my Bridegroom, most beloved, hide Yourself in the inmost depths of my soul, communicating Yourself to it in secret, and manifesting Your hidden wonders which no mortal eyes may see.

"Turn Your face to the mountains."

3. The face of God is His divinity. The mountains are the powers of the soul, memory, understanding, and will. Thus the meaning of these words is: Enlighten my understanding with Your Divinity, and give it the divine intelligence, fill my will with divine love, and my memory with divine possession of glory. The bride here prays for all that may be prayed for; for she is not content with that knowledge of God once granted to Moses [173] -- the knowledge of Him by His works -- for she prays to see the face of God, which is the essential communication of His Divinity to the soul, without any intervening medium, by a certain knowledge thereof in the Divinity. This is something beyond sense, and divested of accidents, inasmuch as it is the contact of pure substances -- that is, of the soul and the Divinity.

"Do not speak."

4. That is, do not speak as before, when Your conversation with me was known to the outward senses, for it was once such as to be comprehended by them; it was not so profound but they could fathom it. Now let Your conversation with me be so deep and so substantial, and so interior, as to be above the reach of the senses; for the substance of the spirit is incommunicable to sense, and the communication made through the senses, especially in this life, cannot be purely spiritual, because the senses are not capable of it. The soul, therefore, longing for that substantial and essential communication of God, of which sense cannot be cognizant, prays the Bridegroom not to speak: that is to say, let the deep secret of the spiritual union be such as to escape the notice of the senses, like the secret which St. Paul heard, and which it is not lawful for a man to speak. [174]

"But regard the companions."

5. The regard of God is love and grace. The companions here are the many virtues of the soul, its gifts, perfections, and other spiritual graces with which God has endowed it; pledges, tokens, and presents of its betrothal. Thus the meaning of the words seems to be this: "Turn Your face to the interior of my soul, O my Beloved; be enamored of the treasures which You have laid up there, so that, enamored of them, You may hide Yourself among them and there dwell; for in truth, though they are

Yours, they are mine also, because You have given them."

"Of her who travels amidst strange islands."

6. That is, "Of my soul tending towards You through strange knowledge of You, by strange ways" -- strange to sense and to the ordinary perceptions of nature. It is as if the bride said, by way of constraining Him to yield: "Seeing that my soul is tending towards You through knowledge which is spiritual, strange, unknown to sense, also communicate Yourself to it so interiorly and so profoundly that the senses may not observe it."

NOTE

IN order to the attainment of a state of perfection so high as this of the spiritual marriage, the soul that aims at it must not only be purified and cleansed from all the imperfections, rebellions, and imperfect habits of the inferior part, which is now -- the old man being put away -- subject and obedient to the higher, but it must also have great courage and most exalted love for so strong and close an embrace of God. For in this state the soul not only attains to exceeding pureness and beauty, but also acquires a terrible strength by reason of that strict and close bond which in this union binds it to God. The soul, therefore, in order to reach this state must have purity, strength, and adequate love. The Holy Spirit, the author of this spiritual union, desirous that the soul should attain thus far in order to merit it, addresses Himself to the Father and the Son, saying: "Our sister is little, and has no breasts. What shall we do to our sister in the day when she is to be spoken to? If she is a wall, let us build upon it bulwarks of silver; if she is a door, let us join it together with boards of cedar." [175]

2. The "bulwarks of silver" are the strong heroic virtues comprised in the faith, which is signified by silver, and these heroic virtues are those of the spiritual marriage, which are built upon the soul, signified by the wall, relying on the strength of which, the peaceful Bridegroom reposes undisturbed by any infirmities. The "boards of cedar" are the affections and accessories of this deep love which is signified by the cedar-tree, and this is the love of the spiritual marriage. In order "to join it together," that is, to adorn the bride, it is necessary she should be the door for the Bridegroom to enter through, keeping the door of the will open in a perfect and true consent of love, which is the consent of the betrothal given previous to the spiritual marriage. The breasts of the bride are also this perfect love which she must have in order to appear in the presence of Christ her Bridegroom for the perfection of such a state.

3. It is written in the Canticle that the bride in her longing for this presence immediately replied, saying: "I am a wall: and my breasts are as a tower" -- that is, "My soul is strong, and my love most deep" -- that He may not fail her on that ground. The bride, too, had expressed as much in the preceding stanzas, out of the fullness of her longing for the perfect union and transformation, and particularly in the last, wherein she set before the Bridegroom all the virtues, graces, and good dispositions with which she was adorned by Him, and that with the object of making Him the prisoner of her love.

4. Now the Bridegroom, to bring this matter to a close, replies in the two stanzas that follow, which describe Him as perfectly purifying the soul, strengthening and disposing it, both as to its sensual and spiritual part, for this state, and charging all resistance and rebellion, both of the flesh and of the devil, to cease, saying:

Footnotes:

173. Exod. 33:23
174. 2 Cor. 12:4
175. Cant. 8:8

A Spiritual Canticle of the Soul and the Bridegroom Christ

STANZAS XX, XXI

THE BRIDEGROOM

> Light-winged birds,
> Lions, fawns, bounding does,
> Mountains, valleys, strands,
> Waters, winds, heat,
> And the terrors that keep watch by night;
> By the soft lyres
> And the siren strains, I adjure you,
> Let your fury cease,
> And touch not the wall,
> That the bride may sleep in greater security.

HERE the Son of God, the Bridegroom, leads the bride into the enjoyment of peace and tranquillity in the conformity of her lower to her higher nature, purging away all her imperfections, subjecting the natural powers of the soul to reason, and mortifying all her desires, as it is expressed in these two stanzas, the meaning of which is as follows. In the first place the Bridegroom adjures and commands all vain distractions of the fancy and imagination from henceforth to cease, and controls the irascible and concupiscible faculties which were previously the sources of so much affliction. He brings, so far as it is possible in this life, the three powers of memory, understanding, and will to the perfection of their objects, and then adjures and commands the four passions of the soul, joy, hope, grief, and fear, to be still, and bids them from henceforth be moderate and calm.

2. All these passions and faculties are comprehended under the expressions employed in the first stanza, the operations of which, full of trouble, the Bridegroom subdues by that great sweetness, joy, and courage which the bride enjoys in the spiritual surrender of Himself to her which God makes at this time; under the influence of which, because God transforms the soul effectually in Himself, all the faculties, desires, and movements of the soul lose their natural imperfection and become divine.

"Light-winged birds."

3. These are the distractions of the imagination, light and rapid in their flight from one subject to another. When the will is tranquilly enjoying the sweet conversation of the Beloved, these distractions produce weariness, and in their swift flight quench its joy. The Bridegroom adjures them by the soft lyres. That is, now that the sweetness of the soul is so abundant and so continuous that they cannot interfere with it, as they did before when it had not reached this state, He adjures them, and bids them cease from their disquieting violence. The same explanation is to be given of the rest of the stanza.

"Lions, fawns, bounding does."

4. By the lions is meant the raging violence of the irascible faculty, which in its acts is bold and daring as a lion. The "fawns and bounding does" are the concupiscible faculty -- that is, the power of desire, the qualities of which are two, timidity and rashness. Timidity betrays itself when things do not turn out according to our wishes, for then the mind retires within itself discouraged, and in this respect the soul resembles the fawns. For as fawns have the concupiscible faculty stronger than many other animals, so are they more retiring and more timid. Rashness betrays itself when we have our own way, for the mind is then neither retiring nor timid, but desires boldly, and gratifies all its inclinations. This quality of rashness is compared to the does, who so eagerly seek what they desire that they not only run, but even leap after it; hence they are described as bounding does.

5. Thus the Bridegroom, in adjuring the lions, restrains the violence and controls the fury of rage; in adjuring the fawns, He strengthens the concupiscible faculty against timidity and irresolution; and in adjuring the does He satisfies and subdues the desires which were restless before, leaping, like deer,

from one object to another, to satisfy that concupiscence which is now satisfied by the soft lyres, the sweetness of which it enjoys, and by the siren strains, in the delight of which it revels.

6. But the Bridegroom does not adjure anger and concupiscence themselves, because these passions never cease from the soul -- but their vexations and disorderly acts, signified by the "lions, fawns, and bounding does," for it is necessary that these disorderly acts should cease in this state.

"Mountains, valleys, strands."

7. These are the vicious and disorderly actions of the three faculties of the soul -- memory, understanding, and will. These actions are disorderly and vicious when they are in extremes, or, if not in extreme, tending to one extreme or other. Thus the mountains signify those actions which are vicious in excess, mountains being high; the valleys, being low, signify those which are vicious in the extreme of defect. Strands, which are neither high nor low, but, inasmuch as they are not perfectly level, tend to one extreme or other, signify those acts of the three powers of the soul which depart slightly in either direction from the true mean and equality of justice. These actions, though not disorderly in the extreme, as they would be if they amounted to mortal sin, are nevertheless disorderly in part, tending towards venial sin or imperfection, however slight that tendency may be, in the understanding, memory, and will. He adjures also all these actions which depart from the true mean, and bids them cease before the soft lyres and the siren strains, which so effectually charm the powers of the soul as to occupy them completely in their true and proper functions, so that they avoid not only all extremes, but also the slightest tendency to them.

"Waters, winds, heat, and the terrors that keep watch by night."

8. These are the affections of the four passions, grief, hope, joy, and fear. The waters are the affections of grief which afflict the soul, for they rush into it like water. "Save me, O God," says the Psalmist, "for the waters have come in even to my soul." [176] The winds are the affections of hope, for they rush forth like wind, desiring what which is not present but hoped for, as the Psalmist says: "I opened my mouth and drew breath: because I longed for Your commandments." [177] That is, "I opened the mouth of my hope, and drew in the wind of desire, because I hoped and longed for Your commandments." Heat is the affections of joy which, like fire, inflame the heart, as it is written: "My heart waxed hot within me; and in my meditation a fire shall burn"; [178] that is, "while I meditate I shall have joy."

9. The "terrors that keep watch by night" are the affections of fear, which in spiritual persons who have not attained to the state of spiritual marriage are usually exceedingly strong. They come sometimes from God when He is going to bestow certain great graces upon souls, as I said before; [179] He is wont then to fill the mind with dread, to make the flesh tremble and the senses numb, because nature is not made strong and perfect and prepared for these graces. They come also at times from the evil spirit, who, out of envy and malignity, when he sees a soul sweetly recollected in God, labors to disturb its tranquillity by exciting horror and dread, in order to destroy so great a blessing, and sometimes utters his threats, as it were in the interior of the soul. But when he finds that he cannot penetrate within the soul, because it is so recollected, and so united with God, he strives at least in the province of sense to produce exterior distractions and inconstancy, sensible pains and horrors, if perchance he may in this way disturb the soul in the bridal chamber.

10. These are called terrors of the night, because they are the work of evil spirits, and because Satan labors, by the help thereof, to involve the soul in darkness, and to obscure the divine light wherein it rejoices. These terrors are called watchers, because they awaken the soul and rouse it from its sweet interior slumber, and also because Satan, their author, is ever on the watch to produce them. These terrors strike the soul of persons who are already spiritual, passively, and come either from God or the evil spirit. I do not refer to temporal or natural terrors, because spiritual men are not subject to these, as they are to those of which I am speaking.

11. The Beloved adjures the affections of these four passions, compels them to cease and to be at rest, because He supplies the bride now with force, and courage, and satisfaction, by the soft lyres of His sweetness and the siren strains of His delight, so that not only they shall not domineer over the soul, but shall not occasion it any distaste whatever. Such is the grandeur and stability of the soul in this state, that, although formerly the waters of grief overwhelmed it, because of its own or other men's sins -- which is what spiritual persons most feel -- the consideration of them now excites neither pain nor annoyance; even the sensible feeling of compassion no longer exists, though the effects of it continue in perfection. The weaknesses of its virtues are no longer in the soul, for they are now constant, strong, and perfect. As the angels perfectly appreciate all sorrowful things without the sense of pain, and perform acts of mercy without the sentiment of pity, so the soul in this transformation of love. God, however, dispenses sometimes, on certain occasions, with the soul in this matter, allowing it to feel and suffer,

A Spiritual Canticle of the Soul and the Bridegroom Christ

that it may become more fervent in love, and grow in merit, or for some other reasons, as He dispensed with His Virgin Mother, St. Paul, and others. This, however, is not the ordinary condition of this state.

12. Neither do the desires of hope afflict the soul now, because, satisfied in its union with God, so far as it is possible in this life, it has nothing of this world to hope for, and nothing spiritual to desire, seeing that it feels itself to be full of the riches of God, though it may grow in charity, and thus, whether living or dying, it is conformed to the will of God, saying with the sense and spirit, "Your will be done," free from the violence of inclination and desires; and accordingly even its longing for the beatific vision is without pain.

13. The affections of joy, also, which were wont to move the soul with more or less vehemence, are not sensibly diminished; neither does their abundance occasion any surprise. The joy of the soul is now so abundant that it is like the sea, which is not diminished by the rivers that flow out of it, nor increased by those that empty themselves into it; for the soul is now that fountain of which our Lord said that it is "springing up into life everlasting." [180]

14. I have said that the soul receives nothing new or unusual in this state of transformation; it seems to lose all accidental joy, which is not withheld even from the glorified. That is, accidental joys and sweetness are indeed no strangers to this soul; indeed, those which it ordinarily has cannot be numbered; yet, for all this, as to the substantial communication of the spirit, there is no increase of joy, for that which may occur anew the soul possesses already, and thus what the soul has already within itself is greater than anything that comes anew. Hence, then, whenever any subject of joy and gladness, whether exterior or spiritually interior, presents itself to the soul, the soul immediately starts rejoicing in the riches it possesses already within itself, and the joy it has in them is far greater than any which these new accessions minister, because, in a certain sense, God is become its possession, Who, though He delights in all things, yet in nothing so much as in Himself, seeing that He has all good eminently in Himself. Thus all accessions of joy serve to remind the soul that its real joy is in its interior possessions, rather than in these accidental causes, because, as I have said, the former are greater than the latter.

15. It is very natural for the soul, even when a particular matter gives it pleasure, that, possessing another of greater worth and gladness, it should remember it at once and take its pleasure in it. The accidental character of these spiritual accessions, and the new impressions they make on the soul, may be said to be as nothing in comparison with that substantial source which it has within itself: for the soul which has attained to the perfect transformation, and is full-grown, grows no more in this state by means of these spiritual accessions, as those souls do who have not yet advanced so far. It is a marvelous thing that the soul, while it receives no accessions of delight, should still seem to do so and also to have been in possession of them. The reason is that it is always tasting them anew, because they are ever renewed; and thus it seems to be continually the recipient of new accessions, while it has no need of them whatever.

16. But if we speak of that light of glory which in this, the soul's embrace, God sometimes produces within it, and which is a certain spiritual communion wherein He causes it to behold and enjoy at the same time the abyss of delight and riches which He has laid up within it, there is no language to express any degree of it. As the sun when it shines upon the sea illumines its great depths, and reveals the pearls, and gold, and precious stones therein, so the divine sun of the Bridegroom, turning towards the bride, reveals in a way the riches of her soul, so that even the angels behold her with amazement and say: "Who is she that comes forth as the morning rising, fair as the moon, bright as the sun, terrible as the army of a camp set in array." [181] This illumination adds nothing to the grandeur of the soul, notwithstanding its greatness, because it merely reveals that which the soul already possessed in order that it might rejoice in it.

17. Finally, the terrors that keep watch by night do not come close to her, because of her pureness, courage, and confident trust in God; the evil spirits cannot shroud her in darkness, nor alarm her with terrors, nor disturb her with their violent assaults. Thus nothing can approach her, nothing can molest her, for she has escaped from all created things and entered into God, to the fruition of perfect peace, sweetness, and delight, so far as that is possible in this life. It is to this state that the words of Solomon are applicable: "A secure mind is as it were a continual feast." [182] As in a feast we have the savor of all meat, and the sweetness of all music, so in this feast, which the bride keeps in the bosom of her Beloved, the soul rejoices in all delight, and has the taste of all sweetness. All that I have said, and all that may be said, on this subject, will always fall short of that which passes in the soul which has attained to this blessed state. For when it shall have attained to the peace of God, "which," in the words of the Apostle, "surpasses all understanding," [183] no description of its state is possible.

"By the soft lyres and the siren strains I adjure you."

18. The soft lyres are the sweetness which the Bridegroom communicates to the soul in this state, and by which He makes all its troubles to cease. As the music of lyres fills the soul with sweetness and delight, carries it rapturously out of itself, so that it forgets all its weariness and grief, so in like manner

this sweetness so absorbs the soul that nothing painful can reach it. The Bridegroom says, in substance: "By that sweetness which I give you, let all your bitterness cease." The siren strains are the ordinary joys of the soul. These are called siren strains because, as it is said, the music of the sirens is so sweet and delicious that he who hears it is so rapt and so carried out of himself that he forgets everything. In the same way the soul is so absorbed in, and refreshed by, the delight of this union that it becomes, as it were, charmed against all the vexations and troubles that may assail it; it is to these the next words of the stanza refer:

"Let your fury cease."

19. This is the troubles and anxieties which flow from unruly acts and affections. As anger is a certain violence which disturbs peace, overlapping its bounds, so also all these affections in their motions transgress the bounds of the peace and tranquillity of the soul, disturbing it whenever they touch it. Hence the Bridegroom says:

"And touch not the wall."

20. The wall is the territory of peace and the fortress of virtue and perfections, which are the defenses and protection of the soul. The soul is the garden wherein the Beloved feeds among the flowers, defended and guarded for Him alone. Hence it is called in the Canticle "a garden enclosed."[184] The Bridegroom bids all disorderly emotions not to touch the territory and wall of His garden.

21. "That the bride may sleep in greater security." That is, that she is delighting herself with more sweetness in the tranquillity and sweetness she has in the Beloved. That is to say, that now no door is shut against the soul, and that it is in its power to abandon itself whenever it wills to this sweet sleep of love, according to the words of the Bridegroom in the Canticle, "I adjure you, O daughters of Jerusalem, by the roes and the harts of the fields, that you raise not up nor make the beloved to awake till herself will."[185]

NOTE

THE Bridegroom was so anxious to rescue His bride from the power of the flesh and the devil and to set her free, that, having done so, He rejoices over her like the good shepherd who, having found the sheep that was lost, laid it upon his shoulders rejoicing; like the woman who, having found the money she had lost, after lighting a candle and sweeping the house, called "together her friends and neighbors, saying, Rejoice with me."[186] So this loving Shepherd and Bridegroom of souls shows a marvelous joy and delight when He beholds a soul gained to perfection lying on His shoulders, and by His hands held fast in the longed-for embrace and union. He is not alone in His joy, for He makes the angels and the souls of the blessed partakers of His glory, saying, as in the Canticle, "Go forth, you daughters of Zion, and see king Solomon in the diadem with which his mother crowned him in the day of his betrothal, and in the day of the joy of his heart."[187] He calls the soul His crown, His bride, and the joy of His heart: He carries it in His arms, and as a bridegroom leads it into His bridal chamber, as we shall see in the following stanza.

Footnotes:

176. Ps. 68:2
177. Ps. 118:131
178. Ps. 38:4
179. Stanza xiii sect. 4; xiv sect. 26.
180. John 4:14
181. Cant. 6:9
182. Prov. 15:15
183. Phil. 4:7
184. Cant. 4:12
185. Cant. 3:5
186. Luke 15:5, 8, 9
187. Cant. 3:11

STANZA XXII

The bride has entered
The pleasant and desirable garden,
And there reposes to her heart's content;
Her neck reclining
On the sweet arms of the Beloved.

THE bride having done what she could in order that the foxes may be caught, the north wind cease, the nymphs, hindrances to the desired joy of the state of spiritual marriage, forgo their troublesome importunities, and having also invoked and obtained the favorable wind of the Holy Spirit, which is the right disposition and means for the perfection of this state, it remains for me now to speak of it in the stanza in which the Bridegroom calls the soul His bride, and speaks of two things: 1. He says that the soul, having gone forth victoriously, has entered the delectable state of spiritual marriage, which they had both so earnestly desired. 2. He enumerates the properties of that state, into the fruition of which the soul has entered, namely, perfect repose, and the resting of the neck on the arms of the Beloved.

"The bride has entered."

2. For the better understanding of the arrangement of these stanzas, and of the way by which the soul advances till it reaches the state of spiritual marriage, which is the very highest, and of which, by the grace of God, I am now about to treat, we must keep in mind that the soul, before it enters it, must be tried in tribulations, in sharp mortifications, and in meditation on spiritual things. This is the subject of this canticle till we come to the fifth stanza, beginning with the words, "A thousand graces diffusing." Then the soul enters on the contemplative life, passing through those ways and straits of love which are described in the course of the canticle, till we come to the thirteenth, beginning with "Turn them away, O my Beloved!" This is the moment of the spiritual betrothal; and then the soul advances by the unitive way, the recipient of many and very great communications, jewels and gifts from the Bridegroom as to one betrothed, and grows into perfect love, as appears from the stanzas which follow that beginning with "Turn them away, O my Beloved!" (the moment of betrothal), to the present, beginning with the words:

"The bride has entered."

3. The spiritual marriage of the soul and the Son of God now remains to be accomplished. This is, beyond all comparison, a far higher state than that of betrothal, because it is a complete transformation into the Beloved; whereby they surrender each to the other the entire possession of themselves in the perfect union of love, wherein the soul becomes divine, and, by participation, God, so far as it is in this life. I believe that no soul ever attains to this state without being confirmed in grace, for the faithfulness of both is confirmed; that of God being confirmed in the soul. Hence it follows, that this is the very highest state possible in this life. As by natural marriage there are "two in one flesh," [188] so also in the spiritual marriage between God and the soul there are two natures in one spirit and love, as we learn from St. Paul, who made use of the same metaphor, saying, "He that cleaves to the Lord is one spirit."[189] So, when the light of a star, or of a candle, is united to that of the sun, the light is not that of the star, nor of the candle, but of the sun itself, which absorbs all other light in its own.

4. It is of this state that the Bridegroom is now speaking, saying, "The bride has entered"; that is, out of all temporal and natural things, out of all spiritual affections, ways, and methods, having left on one side, and forgotten, all temptations, trials, sorrows, anxieties and cares, transformed in this embrace.

"The pleasant and desirable garden."

5. That is, the soul is transformed in God, Who is here called the pleasant garden because of the delicious and sweet repose which the soul finds in Him. But the soul does not enter the garden of perfect transformation, the glory and the joy of the spiritual marriage, without passing first through the spiritual betrothal, the mutual faithful love of the betrothed. When the soul has lived for some time as the bride of the Son, in perfect and sweet love, God calls it and leads it into His flourishing garden for the celebration of the spiritual marriage. Then the two natures are so united, what is divine is so communicated to what is human, that, without undergoing any essential change, each seems to be God -- yet not perfectly so in this life, though still in a manner which can neither be described nor conceived.

6. We learn this truth very clearly from the Bridegroom Himself in the Canticle, where He invites the soul, now His bride, to enter this state, saying: "I am come into my garden, O My sister, My bride: I have gathered My myrrh with My aromatic spices." [190] He calls the soul His sister, His bride, for it is such in love by that surrender which it has made of itself before He had called it to the state of spiritual marriage, when, as He says, He gathered His myrrh with His aromatic spices; that is, the fruits of flowers now ripe and made ready for the soul, which are the delights and grandeurs communicated to it by Himself in this state, that is Himself, and for which He is the pleasant and desirable garden.

7. The whole aim and desire of the soul and of God, in all this, is the accomplishment and perfection of this state, and the soul is therefore never weary till it reaches it; because it finds there a much greater abundance and fullness in God, a more secure and lasting peace, and a sweetness incomparably more perfect than in the spiritual betrothal, seeing that it reposes between the arms of such a Bridegroom, Whose spiritual embraces are so real that it, through them, lives the life of God. Now is fulfilled what St. Paul referred to when he said: "I live; now not I, but Christ lives in me." [191] And now that the soul lives a life so happy and so glorious as this life of God, consider what a sweet life it must be -- a life where God sees nothing displeasing, and where the soul finds nothing irksome, but rather the glory and delight of God in the very substance of itself, now transformed in Him.

"And there reposes to her heart's content; her neck reclining on the sweet arms of the Beloved."

8. The neck is the soul's strength, by means of which its union with the Beloved is wrought; for the soul could not endure so close an embrace if it had not been very strong. And as the soul has labored in this strength, practiced virtue, overcome vice, it is fitting that it should rest there from its labors, "her neck reclining on the sweet arms of the Beloved."

9. This reclining of the neck on the arms of God is the union of the soul's strength, or, rather, of the soul's weakness, with the strength of God, in Whom our weakness, resting and transformed, puts on the strength of God Himself. The state of spiritual matrimony is therefore most fitly designated by the reclining of the neck on the sweet arms of the Beloved; seeing that God is the strength and sweetness of the soul, Who guards and defends it from all evil and gives it to taste of all good.

10. Hence the bride in the Canticle, longing for this state, says to the Bridegroom: "Who shall give to me You my brother, sucking the breast of my mother, that I may find You without, and kiss You, and now no man may despise me." [192] By addressing Him as her Brother she shows the equality between them in the betrothal of love, before she entered the state of spiritual marriage. "Sucking the breast of my mother" signifies the drying up of the passions and desires, which are the breasts and milk of our mother Eve in our flesh, which are a bar to this state. The "finding Him without" is to find Him in detachment from all things and from self when the bride is in solitude, spiritually detached, which takes place when all the desires are quenched. "And kiss You" -- that is, be united with the Bridegroom, alone with Him alone.

11. This is the union of the nature of the soul, in solitude, cleansed from all impurity, natural, temporal, and spiritual, with the Bridegroom alone, with His nature, by love only -- that of love which is the only love of the spiritual marriage, wherein the soul, as it were, kisses God when none despises it nor makes it afraid. For in this state the soul is no longer molested, either by the devil, or the flesh, or the world, or the desires, seeing that here is fulfilled what is written in the Canticle: "Winter is now past, the rain is over and gone. The flowers have appeared in our land." [193]

A Spiritual Canticle of the Soul and the Bridegroom Christ
NOTE

WHEN the soul has been raised to the high state of spiritual marriage, the Bridegroom reveals to it, as His faithful consort, His own marvelous secrets most readily and most frequently, for he who truly and sincerely loves hides nothing from the object of his affections. The chief matter of His communications are the sweet mysteries of His incarnation, the ways and means of redemption, which is one of the highest works of God, and so is to the soul one of the sweetest. Though He communicates many other mysteries, He speaks in the following stanza of His incarnation only, as being the chief; and thus addresses the soul in the words that follow:

Footnotes:

188. Gen. 2:24
189. 1 Cor 6:17
190. Cant. 5:1
191. Gal. 2:20
192. Cant. 8:1
193. Cant. 2:11, 12

STANZA XXIII

Beneath the apple-tree
There were you betrothed;
There I gave you My hand,
And you were redeemed
Where your mother was corrupted.

THE Bridegroom tells the soul of the wondrous way of its redemption and betrothal to Himself, by referring to the way in which the human race was lost. As it was by the forbidden tree of paradise that our nature was corrupted in Adam and lost, so it was by the tree of the Cross that it was redeemed and restored. The Bridegroom there stretched forth the hand of His grace and mercy, in His death and passion, "making void the law of commandments" [194] which original sin had placed between us and God.

"Beneath the apple-tree,"

2. That is the wood of the Cross, where the Son of God was conqueror, and where He betrothed our human nature to Himself, and, by consequence, every soul of man. There, on the Cross, He gave us grace and pledges of His love.

"There were you betrothed, there I gave you My hand."

3. "Help and grace, lifting you up out of your base and miserable condition to be My companion and My bride."

"And you were redeemed where your mother was corrupted."

4. "Your mother, human nature, was corrupted in her first parents beneath the forbidden tree, and you were redeemed beneath the tree of the Cross. If your mother at that tree sentenced you to die, I from the Cross have given you life." It is thus that God reveals the order and dispositions of His wisdom: eliciting good from evil, and turning that which has its origin in evil to be an instrument of greater good. This stanza is nearly word for word what the Bridegroom in the Canticle says to the bride: "Under the apple-tree I raised you up: there your mother was corrupted; there she was deflowered that bare you."[195]

5. It is not the betrothal of the Cross that I am speaking of now -- that takes place, once for all, when God gives the first grace to the soul in baptism. I am speaking of the betrothal in the way of perfection, which is a progressive work. And though both are but one, yet there is a difference between them. The latter is effected in the way of the soul, and therefore slowly: the former in the way of God, and therefore at once.

6. The betrothal of which I am speaking is that of which God speaks Himself by the mouth of the prophet Ezekiel, saying: "You were cast out upon the face of the earth in the abjection of your soul, in the day that you were born. And passing by you, I saw that you were trodden under foot in your blood; and I said to you when you were in your blood: Live: I said to you, I say; in your blood live. Multiplied as the spring of the field have I made you; and you were multiplied and made great, and you went in, and came to the ornaments of woman; your breasts swelled and your hair budded: and you were naked and full of confusion. And I passed by you and saw you, and behold, your time, the time of lovers; and I spread My garment over you and covered your ignominy. And I swore to you; and I entered a covenant with you, says the Lord God; and you were made Mine. And I washed you with water, and made clean your blood from off you: and I anointed you with oil. And I clothed you with diverse colors, and shod you with hyacinth, and I girded you with silk and clothed you with fine garments. And I adorned you with ornaments, and put bracelets on your hands, and a chain about your neck. And I put a jewel upon your forehead and rings in your ears, and a crown of beauty on your head. And you were adorned with gold and silver, and were clothed with silk, and embroidered work, and many colors: you ate fine flour, and honey, and oil, and were made beautiful exceedingly, and advanced to be a queen. And your name

A Spiritual Canticle of the Soul and the Bridegroom Christ

went forth among the nations because of your beauty." [196] These are the words of Ezekiel, and this is the state of that soul of which I am now speaking.

NOTE

AFTER the mutual surrender to each other of the bride and the Beloved, comes their bed. Thereon the bride enters into the joy of Christ. Thus the present stanza refers to the bed, which is pure and chaste, and divine, and in which the bride is pure, divine, and chaste. The bed is nothing else but the Bridegroom Himself, the Word, the Son of God, in Whom, through the union of love, the bride reposes. This bed is said to be of flowers, for the Bridegroom is not only that, but, as He says Himself of Himself, "I am the flower of the field and the lily of the valleys." [197] The soul reposes not only on the bed of flowers, but on that very flower which is the Son of God, and which contains in itself the divine odor, fragrance, grace, and beauty, as He says by the mouth of David, "With me is the beauty of the field." [198] The soul, therefore, in the stanza that follows, celebrates the properties and beauties of its bed, saying:

Footnotes:

194. Eph. 2:15
195. Cant. 8:5
196. Ezek. 16:5-14
197. Cant. 2:1
198. Ps. 49:11

STANZA XXIV

THE BRIDE

Our bed is of flowers
By dens of lions encompassed,
Hung with purple,
Made in peace,
And crowned with a thousand shields of gold.

IN two of the foregoing stanzas -- the fourteenth and the fifteenth --the bride-soul celebrated the grace and magnificence of the Beloved, the Son of God. In the present stanza she not only pursues the same subject, but also sings of her high and blessed state, and her own security in it. She then proceeds to the virtues and rich gifts with which she is endowed and adorned in the chamber of the Bridegroom; for she says that she is in union with Him, and is strong in virtue. Next she says that she has attained to the perfection of love, and then that she enjoys perfect spiritual peace, endowed and adorned with gifts and graces, so far as it is possible to have them in this life. The first subject of the stanza is the joy which the bride feels in her union with the Beloved, saying:

"Our bed is of flowers."

2. I have already said that this bed of the soul is the bosom and love of the Son of God, full of flowers to the soul, which now united to God and reposing in Him, as His bride, shares the bosom and love of the Beloved. That is, the soul is admitted to a knowledge of the wisdom, secrets and graces, and gifts and powers of God, whereby it is made so beautiful, so rich, so abounding in delights that it seems to be lying on a bed of many-colored divine flowers, the touch of which makes it thrill with joy, and the odors of which refresh it.

3. This union of love with God is therefore most appropriately called a bed of flowers, and is so called by the bride in the Canticle, saying to the Beloved, "Our bed is of flowers." [199] She speaks of it as ours, because the virtues and the love, one and the same, of the Beloved are common to both together, and the delight of both is one and the same; as it is written: "My delights were to be with the children of men." [200] The bed is said to be of flowers, because in this state the virtues in the soul are perfect and heroic, which they could not be until the bed had flowered in perfect union with God.

"By dens of lions encompassed."

4. The dens of lions signify the virtues with which the soul is endowed in the state of union. The dens of lions are safe retreats, protected from all other animals, who, afraid of the boldness and strength of the lion within, are afraid not only to enter, but even to appear in sight. So each virtue of the soul in the state of perfection is like a den of lions where Christ dwells united to the soul in that virtue; and in every one of them as a strong lion. The soul also, united to Him in those very virtues, is as a strong lion, because it then partakes of the perfections of God.

5. Thus, then, the perfect soul is so defended, so strong in virtue, and in all virtues together, reposing on the flowery bed of its union with God, that the evil spirits are not only afraid to assault it, but even dare not appear before it; such is their dread of it, when they behold it strong, courageous, and mature in its perfect virtues, on the bed of the Beloved. The evil spirits fear a soul transformed in the union of love as much as they fear the Beloved Himself, and they dare not look upon it, for Satan is in great fear of that soul which has attained to perfection.

6. The soul's bed is encompassed by virtues: they are the dens, for when the soul has advanced to perfection, its virtues are so perfectly ordered, and so joined together and bound up one with another, each supporting the other, that no part of it is weak or exposed. Not only is Satan unable to penetrate within it, but even worldly things, whether great or little, fail to disturb or annoy it, or even move it; for being now free from all molestation of natural affections, and a stranger to the worry of temporal anxieties, it enjoys in security and peace the participation of God.

A Spiritual Canticle of the Soul and the Bridegroom Christ

7. This is that for which the bride longed when she said, "Who shall give to me You my brother, sucking the breast of my mother, that I may find You without, and kiss You, and now no man may despise me?" [201] The "kiss" here is the union of which I am speaking, whereby the soul, by love, becomes in a sense the equal of God. This is the object it desires when it says, "Who shall give to me You my brother?" That means and makes equality. "Sucking the breast of my mother"; that is, destroying all the imperfections and desires of nature which the soul inherits from its mother Eve. "That I may find You without"; that is, "be united to You alone, away from all things, in detachment of the will and desires." "And now no man may despise me"; that is, the world, the devil, and the flesh will not venture to assail it, for being free and purified, and also united to God, none of these can molest it. Thus, then, the soul is in the enjoyment now of habitual sweetness and tranquillity that never fail it.

8. But beside this habitual contentment and peace, the flowers of the virtues of this garden so open in the soul and diffuse their odors that it seems to be, and is, full of the delights of God. I say that the flowers open; because the soul, though filled with the virtues in perfection, is not always in the actual fruition of them, notwithstanding its habitual perception of the peace and tranquillity which they produce. We may say of these virtues that they are in this life like the budding flowers of a garden; they offer a most beautiful sight -- opening under the inspirations of the Holy Spirit -- and diffuse most marvelous perfumes in great variety.

9. Sometimes the soul will discern in itself the mountain flowers -- the fullness, grandeur, and beauty of God -- intermingled with the lilies of the valley -- rest, refreshment, and defense; and again among them, the fragrant roses of the strange islands -- the strange knowledge of God; and further, the perfume of the water lilies of the roaring torrents -- the majesty of God filling the whole soul. And amid all this, it enjoys the exquisite fragrance of the jasmine, and the whisper of the amorous gales, the fruition of which is granted to the soul in the estate of union, and in the same way all the other virtues and graces, the calm knowledge, silent music, murmuring solitude, and the sweet supper of love; and the joy of all this is such as to make the soul say in truth, "Our bed is of flowers, by dens of lions encompassed." Blessed is that soul which in this life deserves at times to enjoy the perfume of these divine flowers.

"Hung with purple."

10. Purple in Holy Scripture means charity, and kings are clad in it, and for that reason the soul says that the bed of flowers is hung with purple, because all the virtues, riches, and blessings of it are sustained, flourish, and are delighted only in charity and love of the King of heaven; without that love the soul can never delight in the bed nor in the flowers thereof. All these virtues, therefore, are, in the soul, as if hung on the love of God, as on that which preserves them, and they are, as it were, bathed in love; for all and each of them always make the soul love God, and on all occasions and in all actions they advance in love to a greater love of God. That is what is meant by saying that the bed is hung with purple.

11. This is well expressed in the sacred Canticle: "King Solomon has made himself a litter of the wood of Lebanon; the pillars thereof he has made of silver, the seat of gold, the going up of purple; the midst he has paved with charity." [202] The virtues and graces which God lays in the bed of the soul are signified by the wood of Lebanon: the pillars of silver and the seat of gold are love, for, as I have said, the virtues are maintained by love, and by the love of God and of the soul are ordered and bring forth fruit.

"Made in peace."

12. This is the fourth excellence of the bed, and depends on the third, of which I have just spoken. For the third is perfect charity, the property of which is, as the Apostle says, to cast out fear; [203] hence the perfect peace of the soul, which is the fourth excellence of this bed. For the clearer understanding of this we must keep in mind that each virtue is in itself peaceful, gentle, and strong, and consequently, in the soul which possesses them, produces peace, gentleness, and fortitude. Now, as the bed is of flowers, formed of the flowers of virtues, all of which are peaceful, gentle, and strong, it follows that the bed is wrought in peace, and the soul is peaceful, gentle, and strong, which are three qualities unassailable by the world, Satan, and the flesh. The virtues preserve the soul in such peace and security that it seems to be wholly built up in peace. The fifth property of this bed of flowers is explained in the following words:

"Crowned with a thousand shields of gold."

13. The shields are the virtues and graces of the soul, which, though they are also the flowers, serve for its crown, and the reward of the toil by which they are acquired. They serve also, like strong shields, as a protection against the vices, which it overcame by the practice of them; and the bridal bed of flowers therefore -- that is, the virtues, the crown and defense -- is adorned with them by way of reward, and protected by them as with a shield. The shields are said to be of gold, to show the great worth of the virtues. The bride in the Canticle sets forth the same truth, saying: "Three score valiant men of the most valiant of Israel surround the little bed of Solomon, all holding swords; . . . every man's sword upon his thigh, because of fears in the night." [204]

14. Thus in this stanza the bride speaks of a thousand shields, to express the variety of the virtues, gifts, and graces with which God has endowed the soul in this state. The Bridegroom also in the Canticle has employed the same expression, in order to show forth the innumerable virtues of the soul, saying: "Your neck is as the tower of David, which is built with bulwarks; a thousand shields hang upon it, all the armor of valiant men." [205]

NOTE

THE soul, having attained to perfection, is not satisfied with magnifying and extolling the excellencies of the Beloved, the Son of God, nor with recounting and giving thanks for the graces received at His hands and the joy into which it has entered, but recounts also the graces conferred on other souls. In this blessed union of love the soul is able to contemplate both its own and others' graces; thus praising Him and giving Him thanks for the many graces bestowed upon others, it sings as in the following stanza:

Footnotes:

199. Cant. 1:15
200. Prov. 8:31
201. Cant. 8:1
202. Cant. 3:9, 10
203. 1 John 4:18
204. Cant. 3:7, 8
205. Cant. 4:4

STANZA XXV

In Your footsteps
The young ones run Your way;
At the touch of the fire
And by the spiced wine,
The divine balsam flows.

HERE the bride gives thanks to her Beloved for three graces which devout souls receive from Him, by which they encourage and excite themselves to love God more and more. She speaks of them here because she has had experience of them herself in this state of union. The first is sweetness, which He gives them, and which is so efficacious that it makes them run swiftly on the road of perfection. The second is a visit of love, by which they are suddenly set on fire with love. The third is overflowing charity infused into them, with which He so inebriates them that they are as much excited by it as by the visit of love, to utter the praises of God, and to love Him with all sweetness.

"In Your footsteps."

2. These are the marks on the ground by which we trace the course of one we seek. The sweetness and knowledge of Himself which God communicates to the soul that seeks Him are the footsteps by which it traces and recognizes Him. Thus the soul says to the Word, the Bridegroom, "In Your footsteps" -- "in the traces of Your sweetness which You diffuse, and the odors which You scatter."

"The young ones run Your way."

3. "Devout souls run with youthful vigor in the sweetness which Your footsteps communicate." They run in many ways and in various directions -- each according to the spirit which God bestows and the vocation He has given -- in the diversified forms of spiritual service on the road of everlasting life, which is evangelical perfection, where they meet the Beloved in the union of love, in spiritual detachment from all things.

4. This sweetness and impression of Himself which God leaves in the soul render it light and active in running after Him; for the soul then does little or nothing in its own strength towards running along this road, being rather attracted by the divine footsteps, so that it not only advances, but even runs, as I said before, in many ways. The bride in the Canticle, therefore, prays for the divine attraction, saying, "Draw me, we will run after You to the odor of Your ointments"; [206] and David says, "I have run the way of Your commandments, when You dilated my heart." [207]

"At the touch of the fire, and by the spiced wine, the divine balsam flows."

5. I said, while explaining the previous lines, that souls run in His footsteps in the way of exterior works. But the three lines I have just quoted refer to the interior acts of the will, when souls are under the influence of the other two graces, and interior visits of the Beloved. These are the touch of fire, and spiced wine; and the interior act of the will, which is the result of these visits, is the flowing of the divine balsam. The contact of the fire is that most delicate touch of the Beloved which the soul feels at times even when least expecting it, and which sets the heart on fire with love, as if a spark of fire had fallen upon it and made it burn. Then the will, in an instant, like one roused from sleep, burns with the fire of love, longs for God, praises Him and gives Him thanks, worships and honors Him, and prays to Him in the sweetness of love.

6. This is the flowing of the divine balsam, which obeys the touch of the fire that issues forth from the consuming love of God which that fire kindled; the divine balsam which comforts the soul and heals it with its odor and its substance.

7. The bride in the Canticle speaks of this divine touch, saying, "My Beloved put His hand through the opening, and my belly trembled at His touch." [208] The touch of the Beloved is the touch of love, and His hand is the grace He bestows upon the soul, and the opening through which He puts His hand is the

vocation and the perfection, at least the degree of perfection of the soul; for accordingly will His touch be heavier or lighter, in proportion to its spiritual state. The belly that trembled is the will, in which the touch is effected, and the trembling is the stirring up of the desires and affections to love, long for, and praise God, which is the flowing of the balsam from this touch.

8. "The spiced wine" is that exceedingly great grace which God sometimes bestows upon advanced souls, when the Holy Spirit inebriates them with the sweet, luscious, and strong wine of love. Hence it is here called spiced wine, for as such wine is prepared by fermentation with many and diverse aromatic and strengthening herbs; so this love, the gift of God to the perfect, is in the soul prepared and seasoned with the virtues already acquired. This love, seasoned with the precious spices, communicates to the soul such a strong, abundant inebriation when God visits it that it pours forth with great effect and force those acts of rapturous praise, love, and worship which I referred to before, and that with a marvelous longing to labor and to suffer for Him.

9. This sweet inebriation and grace, however, do not pass quickly away, like the touch of the fire, for they are of longer continuance. The fire touches and passes, but the effects abide often; and sometimes the spiced wine continues for a considerable time, and its effects also; this is the sweet love of the soul, and continues occasionally a day or two, sometimes even many days together, though not always in the same degree of intensity, because it is not in the power of the soul to control it. Sometimes the soul, without any effort of its own, is conscious of a most sweet interior inebriation, and of the divine love burning within, as David says, "My heart waxed hot within me, and in my meditation a fire shall burn." [209]

10. The outpourings of this inebriation last sometimes as long as the inebriation itself. At other times there are no outpourings; and they are more or less intense when they occur, in proportion to the greater or less intensity of the inebriation itself. But the outpourings, or effects of the fire, generally last longer than the fire which caused them; indeed the fire leaves them behind in the soul, and they are more vehement than those which proceed from the inebriation, for sometimes this divine fire burns up and consumes the soul in love.

11. As I have mentioned fermented wine, it will be well to touch briefly upon the difference between it, when it is old, and new wine; the difference between old wine and new wine is the same, and will furnish a little instruction for spiritual men. New wine has not settled on the lees, and is therefore fermenting; we cannot ascertain its quality or worth before it has settled, and the fermentation has ceased, for until then there is great risk of its corruption. The taste of it is rough and sharp, and an immoderate draught of it intoxicates. Old wine has settled on the lees, and ferments no more like new wine; the quality of it is easily ascertained and it is now very safe from corruption, for all fermentation which might have proved pernicious has entirely ceased. Well-fermented wine is very rarely spoiled, the taste of it is pleasant, and its strength is in its own substance, not in the taste, and drinking it produces health and a sound constitution.

12. New lovers are compared to new wine; these are beginners in the service of God, because the fervor of their love manifests itself outwardly in the senses; because they have not settled on the lees of sense, frail and imperfect; and because they measure the strength of love by the sweetness of it, for it is sensible sweetness that ordinarily gives them their strength for good works, and it is by this they are influenced; we must, therefore, place no confidence in this love till the fermentation has subsided, with the coarse satisfaction of sense.

13. For as these fervors and sensible warmth may incline men to good and perfect love, and serve as an excellent means to it, when the lees of imperfections are cleared; so also is it very easy at first, when sensible sweetness is fresh, for the wine of love to fail, and the sweetness of the new to vanish. New lovers are always anxious, sensibly tormented by their love; it is necessary for them to put some restraint upon themselves, for if they are very active in the strength of this wine, their natural powers will be ruined with these anxieties and fatigues of the new wine, which is rough and sharp, and not made sweet in the perfect fermentation, which then takes place when the anxieties of love are over, as I shall show immediately.

14. The Wise Man employs the same illustration; saying, "A new friend is as new wine; it shall grow old, and you shall drink it with pleasure." [210] Old lovers, therefore, who have been tried and proved in the service of the Bridegroom, are like old wine settled on the lees; they have no sensible emotions, nor outbursts of exterior zeal, but they taste the sweetness of the wine of love, now thoroughly fermented, not sweet to the senses as was that of the love of beginners, but rather settled within the soul in the substance and sweetness of the spirit, and in perfect good works. Such souls as these do not seek after sensible sweetness and fervors, neither do they wish for them, lest they should suffer from loathing and weariness; for he who gives the reins to his desires in matters of sense must of necessity suffer pain and loathing, both in mind and body.

15. Old lovers, therefore, free from that spiritual sweetness which has its roots in the senses, suffer neither in sense nor spirit from the anxieties of love, and thus scarcely ever prove faithless to God, because they have risen above that which might be an occasion of falling, namely, the flesh. These now

A Spiritual Canticle of the Soul and the Bridegroom Christ

drink of the wine of love, which is not only fermented and free from the lees, but spiced also with the aromatic herbs of perfect virtues, which will not allow it to corrupt, as may happen to new wine.

16. For this cause an old friend is of great price in the eyes of God: "Forsake not an old friend, for the new will not be like to him." [211] It is through this wine of love, tried and spiced, that the divine Beloved produces in the soul that divine inebriation, under the influence of which it sends forth to God the sweet and delicious outpourings. The meaning of these three lines, therefore, is as follows: "At the touch of the fire, by which You stir up the soul, and by the spiced wine with which You do so lovingly inebriate it, the soul pours forth the acts and movements of love which are Your work within it."

NOTE

SUCH, then, is the state of the blessed soul in the bed of flowers, where all these blessings, and many more, are granted it. The seat of that bed is the Son of God, and the hangings of it are the charity and love of the Bridegroom Himself. The soul now may say, with the bride, "His left hand is under my head," [212] and we may therefore say, in truth, that such a soul is clothed in God, and bathed in the Divinity, and that, not as it were on the surface, but in the interior spirit, and filled with the divine delights in the abundance of the spiritual waters of life; for it experiences that which David says of those who have drawn near to God: "They shall be inebriated with the plenty of Your house, and You shall make them drink of the torrent of Your pleasure, for with You is the fountain of life." [213]

2. This fullness will be in the very being of the soul, seeing that its drink is nothing else but the torrent of delights, and that torrent the Holy Spirit, as it is written: "And he showed me a river of living water, clear as crystal, proceeding from the throne of God and the Lamb." [214] This water, being the very love itself of God, flows into the soul, so that it drinks of the torrent of love, which is the spirit of the Bridegroom infused into the soul in union. Thence the soul in the overflowing of its love sings the following stanza:

Footnotes:

206. Cant. 1:3
207. Ps. 118:32
208. Cant. 5:4
209. Ps. 38:4
210. Ecclus. 9:15
211. Ecclus. 9:14
212. Cant. 2:6
213. Ps. 35:9
214. Rev. 22:1

STANZA XXVI

In the inner cellar
Of my Beloved have I drunk; and when I went forth
Over all the plain
I knew nothing,
And lost the flock I followed before.

HERE the soul speaks of that sovereign grace of God in taking it to Himself into the house of His love, which is the union, or transformation of love in God. It describes two effects proceeding therefrom: forgetfulness of, and detachment from, all the things of this world, and the mortification of its tastes and desires.

"In the inner cellar."

2. In order to explain in any degree the meaning of this, I have need of the special help of the Holy Spirit to direct my hand and guide my pen. The cellar is the highest degree of love to which the soul may attain in this life, and is therefore said to be the inner. It follows from this that there are other cellars not so interior; that is, the degrees of love by which souls reach this, the last. These cellars are seven in number, and the soul has entered into them all when it has in perfection the seven gifts of the Holy Spirit, so far as it is possible for it. When the soul has the spirit of fear in perfection, it has in perfection also the spirit of love, inasmuch as this fear, the last of the seven gifts, is filial fear, and the perfect fear of a son proceeds from his perfect love of his father. Thus when the Holy Scripture speaks of one as having perfect charity, it says of him that he fears God. So the prophet Isaiah, announcing the perfections of Christ, says of Him, "The spirit of the fear of the Lord shall replenish him." [215] Holy Simeon also is spoken of by the Evangelist as a "just man full of fear," [216] and the same applies to many others.

3. Many souls reach and enter the first cellar, each according to the perfection of its love, but the last and inmost cellar is entered by few in this world, because therein is wrought the perfect union with God, the union of the spiritual marriage, of which the soul is now speaking. What God communicates to the soul in this intimate union is utterly ineffable, beyond the reach of all possible words -- just as it is impossible to speak of God Himself so as to convey any idea of what He is -- because it is God Himself who communicates Himself to the soul now in the marvelous bliss of its transformation. In this state God and the soul are united, as the window is with the light, or coal with the fire, or the light of the stars with that of the sun, yet, however, not so essentially and completely as it will be in the life to come. The soul, therefore, to show what it received from the hands of God in the cellar of wine, says nothing else, and I do not believe that anything could be said but the words which follow:

"Of my Beloved have I drunk."

4. As a draught diffuses itself through all the members and veins of the body, so this communication of God diffuses itself substantially in the whole soul, or rather, the soul is transformed in God. In this transformation the soul drinks of God in its very substance and its spiritual powers. In the understanding it drinks wisdom and knowledge, in the will the sweetest love, in the memory refreshment and delight in the thought and sense of its bliss. That the soul receives and drinks delight in its very substance, appears from the words of the bride in the Canticle: "My soul melted as He spoke"[217] -- that is, when the Bridegroom communicated Himself to the soul.

5. That the understanding drinks wisdom is evident from the words of the bride longing and praying for the kiss of union: "There You shall teach me, and I will give you a cup of spiced wine."[218] "You shall teach me wisdom and knowledge in love, and I will give You a cup of spiced wine -- that is, my love mingled with Yours." The bride says that the will also drinks of love, saying: "He brought me into the cellar of wine; He has ordered in me charity," [219] -- that is, "He gave me His love, embracing me, to drink of love"; or, to speak more clearly, "He ordered in me His charity, tempering His charity and to the purpose making it mine." This is to give the soul to drink of the very love of its Beloved,

A Spiritual Canticle of the Soul and the Bridegroom Christ
which the Beloved infuses into it.

6. There is a common saying that the will cannot love that of which the understanding has no knowledge. This, however, is to be understood in the order of nature, it being impossible, in a natural way, to love anything unless we first know what it is we love. But in a supernatural way God can certainly infuse love and increase it without infusing and increasing distinct knowledge, as is evident from the texts already quoted. Yes, many spiritual persons have experience of this; their love of God burns more and more, while their knowledge does not grow. Men may know little and love much, and on the other hand, know much and love but little.

7. In general, those spiritual persons whose knowledge of God is not very great are usually very rich in all that belongs to the will, and infused faith suffices them for this knowledge, by means of which God infuses and increases charity in them and the acts thereof, which are to love Him more and more though knowledge is not increased. Thus the will may drink of love while the understanding drinks in no fresh knowledge. In the present instance, however, all the powers of the soul together, because of the union in the inner cellar, drink of the Beloved.

8. As to the memory, it is clear that the soul drinks of the Beloved in it, because it is enlightened with the light of the understanding in remembering the blessings it possesses and enjoys in union with the Beloved.

"And when I went forth."

9. That is, after this grace: the divine draught having so deified the soul, exalted it, and inebriated it in God. Though the soul is always in the high estate of marriage ever since God has placed it there, nevertheless actual union in all its powers is not continuous, though the substantial union is. In this substantial union the powers of the soul are most frequently in union, and drink of His cellar, the understanding by knowledge, the will by love, etc. We are not, therefore, to suppose that the soul, when saying that it went out, has ceased from its substantial or essential union with God, but only from the union of its faculties, which is not, and cannot be, permanent in this life; it is from this union, then, it went forth when it wandered over all the plain -- that is, through the whole breadth of the world.

"I knew nothing."

10. This draught of God's most deep wisdom makes the soul forget all the things of this world, and consider all its previous knowledge, and the knowledge of the whole world besides, as pure ignorance in comparison with this knowledge.

11. For a clearer understanding of this, we must remember that the most regular cause of the soul's ignoring the things of the world, when it has ascended to this high state, is that it is informed by a supernatural knowledge, in the presence of which all natural and worldly knowledge is ignorance rather than knowledge. For the soul in possession of this knowledge, which is most profound, learns from it that all other knowledge not included in this knowledge is not knowledge, but ignorance, and worthless. We have this truth in the words of the Apostle when he said that "the wisdom of this world is foolishness with God." [220]

12. This is the reason why the soul says it knows nothing, now that it has drunk of the divine wisdom. The truth is that the wisdom of men and of the whole world is mere ignorance, and not deserving any attention, but it is a truth that can be learned only in that truth of the presence of God in the soul communicating to it His wisdom and making it strong by this draught of love that it may see it distinctly. This is taught us by Solomon, saying: "The vision that the man spoke, with whom God is, and who being strengthened by God abiding with him, said: I am the most foolish of men, and the wisdom of men is not with me." [221]

13. When the soul is raised to this high wisdom of God, the wisdom of man is in its eyes the lowest ignorance: all natural science and the works of God, if accompanied by ignorance of Him, are as ignorance; for where He is not known, there nothing is known. "The deep things of God are foolishness to men." [222] Thus the divinely wise and the worldly wise are fools in the estimation of each other; for the latter cannot understand the wisdom and science of God, nor the former those of the world, for the wisdom of the world is ignorance in comparison with the wisdom of God; and the wisdom of God is ignorance with respect to that of the world.

14. Moreover, this deification and elevation of the spirit in God, whereby the soul is, as it were, rapt and absorbed in love, one with God, suffer it not to dwell upon any worldly matter. The soul is now detached, not only from all outward things, but even from itself: it is, as it were, undone, assumed by, and dissolved in, love -- that is, it passes out of itself into the Beloved. Thus the bride, in the Canticle, after speaking of her own transformation by love into the Beloved, expresses her state of ignorance by the words "I knew not." [223] The soul is now, in a certain sense, like Adam in paradise, who knew no evil. It is so innocent that it sees no evil; neither does it consider anything to be amiss. It will hear much

that is evil, and will see it with its eyes, and yet it shall not be able to understand it, because it has no evil habits whereby to judge of it. God has rooted out of it those imperfect habits and that ignorance resulting from the evil of sin, by the perfect habit of true wisdom. Thus, also, the soul knows nothing on this subject.

15. Such a soul will scarcely intermeddle with the affairs of others, because it forgets even its own; for the work of the Spirit of God in the soul in which He dwells is to incline it to ignore those things which do not concern it, especially such as do not minister to edification. The Spirit of God abides within the soul to withdraw it from outward things rather than to lead it among them; and thus the soul knows nothing as it knew it formerly. We are not, however, to suppose that it loses the habits of knowledge previously acquired, for those habits are improved by the more perfect habit of supernatural knowledge infused, though these habits are not so powerful as to necessitate knowledge through them, and yet there is no reason why they should not do so occasionally.

16. In this union of the divine wisdom, these habits are united with the higher wisdom of other knowledge, as a little light with another which is great; it is the great light that shines, overwhelming the less, yet the latter is not therefore lost, but rather perfected, though it is not the light which shines pre-eminently. Thus, I imagine, will it be in heaven; the acquired habits of knowledge in the just will not be destroyed, though they will be of no great importance there, seeing that the just will know more in the divine wisdom than by the habits acquired on earth.

17. But the particular notions and forms of things, acts of the imagination, and every other apprehension having form and figure are all lost and ignored in this absorbing love, and this for two reasons. First, the soul cannot actually attend to anything of the kind, because it is actually absorbed by this draught of love. Secondly, and this is the principal reason, its transformation in God so conforms it to His purity and simplicity -- for there is no form or imaginary figure in Him -- as to render it pure, cleansed and empty of all the forms and figures it entertained before, being now purified and enlightened in simple contemplation. All spots and stains in the glass become invisible when the sun shines upon it, but they appear again as soon as the light of the sun is withheld.

18. So is it with the soul; while the effects of this act of love continue, this ignorance continues also, so that it cannot observe anything in particular until these effects have ceased. Love has set the soul on fire and transmuted it into love, has annihilated it and destroyed it as to all that is not love, according to the words of David: "My heart has been inflamed, and my reins have been changed; and I am brought to nothing, and I knew not." [224] The changing of the reins, because the heart is inflamed, is the changing of the soul, in all its desires and actions, in God, into a new manner of life, the utter undoing and annihilation of the old man, and therefore the prophet said that he was brought to nothing and knew not.

19. These are the two effects of drinking the wine of the cellar of God; not only is all previous knowledge brought to nothing and made to vanish, but the old life also with its imperfections is destroyed, and into the new man renewed; this is the second of the two effects described in the words that follow:

"And lost the flock I followed before."

20. Until the soul reaches the state of perfection, however spiritual it may be, there always remains a troop of desires, likings, and other imperfections, sometimes natural, sometimes spiritual, after which it runs, and which it tries to feed while following and satisfying them. With regard to the understanding, there are certain imperfections of the desire of knowledge. With regard to the will, certain likings and peculiar desires, at times in temporal things, as the wish to possess certain trifles, and attachment to some things more than to others, certain prejudices, considerations, and punctilios, with other vanities, still savoring of the world: and again in natural things, such as eating and drinking, the preference of one kind of food over another, and the choice of the best: at another time, in spiritual things, such as seeking for sweetness, and other follies of spiritual persons not yet perfect, too numerous to recount here. As to the memory, there are many inconsistencies, anxieties, unseemly reminiscences, which drag the soul captive after them.

21. The four passions of the soul also involve it in many useless hopes, joys, griefs, and fears, after which it runs. As to this flock, some men are more influenced by it than others; they run after and follow it, until they enter the inner cellar, where they lose it altogether, being then transformed in love. In that cellar the flock of imperfections is easily destroyed, as rust and mold on metal in the fire. Then the soul feels itself free from the pettiness of self-likings and the vanities after which it ran before, and may well say, "I have lost the flock which I followed before."

A Spiritual Canticle of the Soul and the Bridegroom Christ
NOTE

GOD communicates Himself to the soul in this interior union with a love so intense that the love of a mother, who so tenderly caresses her child, the love of a brother, or the affection of a friend bear no likeness to it, for so great is the tenderness, and so deep is the love with which the Infinite Father comforts and exalts the humble and loving soul. O wonders worthy of all awe and reverence! He humbles Himself in reality before that soul that He may exalt it, as if He were its servant, and the soul His lord. He is as anxious to comfort it as if He were a slave, and the soul God. So great is the humility and tenderness of God. In this communion of love He renders in a certain way those services to the soul which He says in the Gospel He will perform for the elect in heaven. "Amen, I say to you, that He will gird Himself and make them sit down to meat, and passing will minister to them."[225]

2. This very service He renders now to the soul, comforting and cherishing it, as a mother her child whom she nurtures in her bosom. And the soul recognizes herein the truth of the words of Isaiah, "You shall be carried at the breasts, and upon the knees they shall caress you."[226] What must the feelings of the soul be amid these sovereign graces? How it will melt away in love, beholding the bosom of God opened for it with such overflowing love. When the soul perceives itself in the midst of these delights, it surrenders itself wholly to God, gives to Him the breasts of its own will and love, and under the influence thereof addresses the Beloved in the words of the bride in the Canticle, saying: "I to my Beloved, and His turning is towards me. Come, my Beloved, let us go forth into the field, let us abide in the villages. Let us rise early to the vineyards, let us see if the vineyard flourish, if the flowers are ready to bring forth fruits, if the pomegranates flourish; there will I give You my breasts"[227] -- that is, "I will employ all the joy and strength of my will in the service of Your love." This mutual surrender in this union of the soul and God is the subject of the stanza which follows:

Footnotes:

215. Isa. 11:3
216. Luke 2:25. Justus et timoratus.
217. Cant. 5:6
218. Cant. 8:2
219. Cant. 2:4
220. 1 Cor. 3:19
221. Prov. 30:1, 2
222. 1 Cor. 2:14
223. Cant. 6:11
224. Ps. 72:21, 22
225. Luke 12:37
226. Isa. 66:12
227. Cant. 7:10-12

St. John of the Cross

STANZA XXVII

There He gave me His breasts,
There He taught me the science full of sweetness.
And there I gave to Him
Myself without reserve;
There I promised to be His bride.

HERE the soul speaks of the two contracting parties in this spiritual betrothal, itself and God. In the inner cellar of love they both met together, God giving to the soul the breasts of His love freely, whereby He instructs it in His mysteries and wisdom, and the soul also actually surrendering itself, making no reservation whatever either in its own favor or in that of others, promising to be His for ever.

"There He gave me His breasts."

2. To give the breast to another is to love and cherish him and communicate one's secrets to him as a friend. The soul says here that God gave it His breasts -- that is, He gave it His love and communicated His secrets to it. It is thus that God deals with the soul in this state, and more, too, as it appears from the words that follow:

"There He taught me the science full of sweetness."

3. This science is mystical theology, which is the secret science of God, and which spiritual men call contemplation. It is most full of sweetness because it is knowledge by love, love is the master of it, and it is love that renders it all so sweet. Inasmuch as this science and knowledge are communicated to the soul in that love with which God communicates Himself, it is sweet to the understanding, because knowledge belongs to it, and sweet to the will, because it comes by love which belongs to the will.

"There I gave to Him myself without reserve"

4. The soul in this sweet draught of God, surrenders itself wholly to Him most willingly and with great sweetness; it desires to be wholly His, and never to retain anything which is unbecoming His Majesty. God is the author of this union, and of the purity and perfection requisite for it; and as the transformation of the soul in Himself makes it His, He empties it of all that is alien to Himself. Thus it comes to pass that, not in will only, but in act as well, the whole soul is entirely given to God without any reserve whatever, as God has given Himself freely to it. The will of God and of the soul are both satisfied, each given up to the other, in mutual delight, so that neither fails the other in the faith and constancy of the betrothal; therefore the soul says:

"There I promised to be His bride."

5. As a bride does not give her love to another, and as all her thoughts and actions are directed to her bridegroom only, so the soul now has no affections of the will, no acts of the understanding, neither object nor occupation of any kind which it does not wholly refer to God, together with all its desires. The soul is, as it were, absorbed in God, and even its first movements have nothing in them -- so far as it can comprehend them -- which is at variance with the will of God. The first movements of an imperfect soul in general are, at least, inclined to evil, in the understanding, the memory, the will, the desires and imperfections; but those of the soul which has attained to the spiritual state of which I am speaking are ordinarily directed to God, because of the great help and courage it derives from Him, and its perfect conversion to goodness. This is set forth with great clearness by David, when he says: "Shall not my soul be subject to God? For from Him is my salvation. For He is my God and my Savior; He is my protector, I shall be moved no more." [228] "He is my protector" means that the soul, being now received under the protection of God and united to Him, is no longer subject to any movements contrary

A Spiritual Canticle of the Soul and the Bridegroom Christ
to God.

6. It is quite clear from this that the soul which has attained the spiritual betrothal knows nothing else but the love of the Bridegroom and the delights thereof, because it has arrived at perfection, the form and substance of which is love, according to St. Paul. [229] The more a soul loves, the more perfect it is in its love, and hence it follows that the soul which is already perfect is, if we may say so, all love, all its actions are love, all its energies and strength are occupied in love. It gives up all it has, like the wise merchant, [230] for this treasure of love which it finds hidden in God, and which is so precious in His sight, and the Beloved cares for nothing else but love; the soul, therefore, anxious to please Him perfectly, occupies itself wholly in pure love for God, not only because love does so occupy it, but also because the love wherein it is united influences it towards love of God in and through all things. As the bee draws honey from all plants, and makes use of them only for that end, so the soul most easily draws the sweetness of love from all that happens to it; makes all things subserve it towards loving God, whether they are sweet or bitter; and being animated and protected by love, has no sense, feeling, or knowledge, because, as I have said, it knows nothing but love, and in all its occupations, its joy is its love of God. This is explained by the following stanza.

NOTE

I HAVE said that God is pleased with nothing but love; but before I explain this, it will be as well to set forth the grounds on which the assertion rests. All our works, and all our labors, however grand they may be, are nothing in the sight of God, for we can give Him nothing, neither can we by them fulfill His desire, which is the growth of our soul. As to Himself He desires nothing of this, for He has need of nothing, and so, if He is pleased with anything it is with the growth of the soul; and as there is no way in which the soul can grow but in becoming in a manner equal to Him, for this reason He is only pleased with our love. It is the property of love to place him who loves on an equality with the object of his love. Hence the soul, because of its perfect love, is called the bride of the Son of God, which signifies equality with Him. In this equality and friendship all things are common, as the Bridegroom Himself said to His disciples: "I have called you friends, because all things, whatsoever I have heard of my Father, I have made known to you." [231]

Footnotes:

228. Ps. 61:2, 3
229. Col. 3:14
230. Matt. 13:44
231. John 15:15

St. John of the Cross

STANZA XXVIII

My soul is occupied,
And all my substance in His service;
Now I guard no flock,
Nor have I any other employment:
My sole occupation is love.

THE soul, or rather the bride having given herself wholly to the Bridegroom without any reserve whatever, now recounts to the Beloved how she fulfills her task. "My soul and body," she says, "all my abilities and all my capacities, are occupied not with other matters, but with those pertaining to the service of the Bridegroom." She is therefore not seeking her own proper satisfaction, nor the gratification of her own inclinations, neither does she occupy herself in anything whatever which is alien to God; yes, even her communion with God Himself is nothing else but acts of love, inasmuch as she has changed her former mode of conversing with Him into loving.

"My soul is occupied."

2. This refers to the soul's surrender of itself to the Beloved in this union of love, wherein it devotes itself, with all its faculties, understanding, will, and memory, to His service. The understanding is occupied in considering what most tends to His service, in order that it might be accomplished; the will in loving all that is pleasing to God, and in desiring Him in all things; the memory in recalling what ministers to Him, and what may be more pleasing to Him.

"And all my substance in His service."

3. By substance here is meant all that relates to the sensual part of the soul, which includes the body, with all its powers, interior and exterior, together with all its natural capacities -- that is, the four passions, the natural desires, and the whole substance of the soul, all of which is employed in the service of the Beloved, as well as the rational and spiritual part, as I explained in the previous section. As to the body, that is now ordered according to God in all its interior and exterior senses, all the acts of which are directed to God; the four passions of the soul are also under control in Him; for the soul's joy, hope, fear, and grief are conversant with God only; all its appetites, and all its anxieties also, are directed to Him only.

4. The whole substance of the soul is now so occupied with God, so intent upon Him, that its very first movements, even inadvertently, have God for their object and their end. The understanding, memory, and will tend directly to God; the affections, senses, desires and longings, hope and joy, the whole substance of the soul, rise instantly towards God, though the soul is making no conscious efforts in that direction. Such a soul is very often doing the work of God, intent upon Him and the things of God, without thinking or reflecting on what it is doing for Him. The constant and habitual practice of this has deprived it of all conscious reflection, and even of that fervor which it usually had when it began to act. The whole substance of the soul being thus occupied, what follows cannot be but true also.

"Now I guard no flock."

5. "I do not now go after my likings and desires; for having fixed them upon God, I no longer feed or guard them." The soul not only does not guard them now, but has no other occupation than to wait upon God.

"Nor have I any other employment."

6. Before the soul succeeded in effecting this gift and surrender of itself, and of all that belongs to it, to the Beloved, it was entangled in many unprofitable occupations, by which it sought to please itself and others, and it may be said that its occupations of this kind were as many as its habits of

A Spiritual Canticle of the Soul and the Bridegroom Christ
imperfection.

7. To these habits belong that of speaking, thinking, and the doing of things that are useless; and likewise, the not making use of these things according to the requirements of the soul's perfection; other desires also the soul may have, with which it ministers to the desires of others, to which may be referred display, compliments, flattery, human respect, aiming at being well thought of, and the giving pleasure to people, and other useless actions, by which it labored to content them, wasting its efforts herein, and finally all its strength. All this is over, says the soul here, for all its words, thoughts, and works are directed to God, and, conversant with Him, freed from their previous imperfections. It is as if it said: "I follow no longer either my own or other men's likings, neither do I occupy or entertain myself with useless pastimes, or the things of this world."

"My sole occupation is love."

8. "All my occupation now is the practice of the love of God, all the powers of soul and body, memory, understanding, and will, interior and exterior senses, the desires of spirit and of sense, all work in and by love. All I do is done in love; all I suffer, I suffer in the sweetness of love." This is the meaning of David when he said, "I will keep my strength to You." [232]

9. When the soul has arrived at this state all the acts of its spiritual and sensual nature, whether active or passive, and of whatever kind they may be, always occasion an increase of love and delight in God: even the act of prayer and communion with God, which was once carried on by reflections and diverse other methods, is now wholly an act of love. So much so is this the case that the soul may always say, whether occupied with temporal or spiritual things, "My sole occupation is love." Happy life! happy state! and happy the soul which has attained to it! where all is the very substance of love, the joyous delights of the betrothal, when it may truly say to the Beloved with the bride in the Canticle, "The new and the old, my Beloved, have I kept for You" [233] "All that is bitter and painful I keep for Your sake, all that is sweet and pleasant I keep for You." The meaning of the words, for my purpose, is that the soul, in the state of spiritual betrothal, is for the most part living in the union of love -- that is, the will is habitually waiting lovingly on God.

NOTE

IN truth the soul is now lost to all things, and gained only to love, and the mind is no longer occupied with anything else. It is, therefore, deficient in what concerns the active life, and other exterior duties, that it may apply in earnest to the one thing which the Bridegroom has pronounced necessary; [234] and that is waiting upon God, and the continuous practice of His love. So precious is this in the eyes of God that He rebuked Martha because she would withdraw Mary from His feet to occupy her actively in the service of our Lord. Martha thought that she was doing everything herself, and that Mary at the feet of Christ was doing nothing. But it was far otherwise: for there is nothing better or more necessary than love. Thus, in the Canticle, the Bridegroom protects the bride, adjuring the daughters of Jerusalem -- that is, all created things -- not to disturb her spiritual sleep of love, nor to waken her, nor to let her open her eyes to anything till she pleased. "I adjure you, O daughters of Jerusalem, that you do not stir up, nor awake my beloved till she please." [235]

2. Observe, however, that if the soul has not reached the state of unitive love, it is necessary for it to make acts of love, as well in the active as in the contemplative life. But when it has reached it, it is not requisite it should occupy itself in other and exterior duties -- unless they are matters of obligation -- which might hinder, were it but for a moment, the life of love in God, though they may minister greatly to His service; because an instant of pure love is more precious in the eyes of God and the soul, and more profitable to the Church, than all other good works together, though it may seem as if nothing were done. Thus, Mary Magdalene, though her preaching was most edifying, and might have been still more so afterwards, out of the great desire she had to please her Bridegroom and benefit the Church, hid herself, nevertheless, in the desert thirty years, that she might surrender herself entirely to love; for she considered that she would gain more in that way, because an instant of pure love is so much more profitable and important to the Church.

3. When the soul, then, in any degree possesses the spirit of solitary love, we must not interfere with it. We should inflict a grievous wrong upon it, and upon the Church also, if we were to occupy it, were it only for a moment, in exterior or active duties, however important they might be. When God Himself adjures all not to waken it from its love, who shall venture to do so, and be blameless? In a word, it is for this love that we are all created. Let those men of zeal, who think by their preaching and exterior works to convert the world, consider that they would be much more edifying to the Church, and more pleasing to God -- setting aside the good example they would give -- if they would spend at least one half their time in prayer, even though they may have not attained to the state of unitive love. Certainly they would do more, and with less trouble, by one single good work than by a thousand:

St. John of the Cross

because of the merit of their prayer, and the spiritual strength it supplies. To act otherwise is to beat the air, to do little more than nothing, sometimes nothing and occasionally even mischief; for God may give up such persons to vanity, so that they may seem to have done something, when in reality their outward occupations bear no fruit; for it is quite certain that good works cannot be done but in the power of God. O how much might be written on this subject! this, however, is not the place for it.

4. I have said this to explain the stanza that follows, in which the soul replies to those who call in question its holy tranquillity, who will have it wholly occupied with outward duties, that its light may shine before the world: these persons have no conception of the fibers and the unseen root whence the sap is drawn, and which nourish the fruit.

Footnotes:

232. Ps. 58:10
233. Cant. 7:13
234. Luke 10:42
235. Cant. 3:5

A Spiritual Canticle of the Soul and the Bridegroom Christ

STANZA XXIX

> *If then on the common land*
> *I am no longer seen or found,*
> *You will say that I am lost;*
> *That, being enamored,*
> *I lost myself; and yet was found.*

THE soul replies here to a tacit reproach. Worldly people are in the habit of censuring those who give themselves up in earnest to God, regarding them as extravagant, in their withdrawal from the world, and in their manner of life. They say also of them that they are useless for all matters of importance, and lost to everything the world prizes and respects! This reproach the soul meets in the best way; boldly and courageously despising it with everything else that the world can lay to its charge. Having attained to a living love of God, it makes little account of all this; and that is not all: it confesses it itself in this stanza, and boasts that it has committed that folly, and that it is lost to the world and to itself for the Beloved.

2. That which the soul is saying here, addressing itself to the world, is in substance this: "If you see me no longer occupied with the subjects that engrossed me once, with the other pastimes of the world, say and believe that I am lost to them, and a stranger to them, yes, that I am lost of my own choice, seeking my Beloved whom I so greatly love." But that they may see that the soul's loss is gain, and not consider it folly and delusion, it adds that its loss was gain, and that it therefore lost itself deliberately.

"If then on the common I am no longer seen or found."

3. The common is a public place where people assemble for recreation, and where shepherds feed their flocks. By the common here is meant the world in general, where men amuse themselves and feed the herd of their desires. The soul says to the worldly-minded: "If you see me no more where I used to be before I gave myself up wholly to God, look upon me as lost, and say so": the soul rejoices in that and would have men so speak of it.

"Say that I am lost."

4. He who loves is not ashamed before men of what he does for God, neither does he hide it through shame though the whole world should condemn it. He who shall be ashamed to confess the Son of God before men, neglecting to do His work, the Son of God also will be ashamed to acknowledge him before His Father. "He that shall deny Me before men, I will also deny him before My Father Who is in heaven." [236] The soul, therefore, in the courage of its love, glories in what ministers to the honor of the Beloved, in that it has done anything for Him and is lost to the things of the world.

5. But few spiritual persons arrive at this perfect courage and resolution in their conduct. For though some attempt to practice it, and some even think themselves proficient therein, they never entirely lose themselves on certain points connected with the world or self, so as to be perfectly detached for the sake of Christ, despising appearances and the opinion of the world. These can never answer, "Say that I am lost," because they are not lost to themselves, and are still ashamed to confess Christ before men through human respect; these do not therefore really live in Christ.

"That being enamored,"

That is, practicing virtues for the love of God,

"I lost myself; and yet was found."

6. The soul remembers well the words of the Bridegroom in the Gospel: "No man can serve two masters; for either he will hate the one and love the other," [237] and therefore, in order not to lose God, loses all that is not God, that is, all created things, even itself, being lost to all things for the love of Him. He who truly loves makes a shipwreck of himself in all else that he may gain the more in the object of his love. Thus the soul says that it has lost itself -- that is, deliberately, of set purpose.

7. This loss occurs in two ways. The soul loses itself, making no account whatever of itself, but of the Beloved, resigning itself freely into His hands without any selfish views, losing itself deliberately, and seeking nothing for itself. Secondly, it loses itself in all things, making no account of anything save that which concerns the Beloved. This is to lose oneself -- that is, to be willing that others should have all things. Such is he that loves God; he seeks neither gain nor reward, but only to lose all, even himself, according to God's will; this is what such a one counts gain. This is real gain, for the Apostle says, "to die is gain" [238] -- that is, to die for Christ is my gain and profit spiritually. This is why the soul says that it "was found"; for he who does not know how to lose, does not find, but rather loses himself, as our Savior teaches us in the Gospel, saying, "He that will save his life shall lose it; and he that shall lose his life for My sake shall find it." [239]

8. But if we wish to know the deeper spiritual meaning of this line, and its peculiar fitness here, it is as follows: When a soul has advanced so far on the spiritual road as to be lost to all the natural methods of communing with God; when it seeks Him no longer by meditation, images, impressions, nor by any other created ways, or representations of sense, but only by rising above them all, in the joyful communion with Him by faith and love, then it may be said to have found God of a truth, because it has truly lost itself as to all that is not God, and also as to its own self.

NOTE

THE soul being thus gained, all its works are gain, for all its powers are exerted in the spiritual intercourse of most sweet interior love with the Beloved. The interior communications between God and the soul are now so delicious, so full of sweetness, that no mortal tongue can describe them, nor human understanding comprehend them. As a bride on the day of her betrothal attends to nothing but to the joyous festival of her love, and brings forth all her jewels and ornaments for the pleasure of the bridegroom, and as he too in the same way exhibits his own magnificence and riches for the pleasure of his bride, so is it in the spiritual betrothal where the soul feels that which the bride says in the Canticle, "I to my Beloved and my Beloved to me." [240] The virtues and graces of the bride-soul, the grandeur and magnificence of the Bridegroom, the Son of God, come forth into the light, for the celebration of the bridal feast, communicating each to the other the goods and joys with the wine of sweet love in the Holy Spirit. The present stanza, addressed to the Bridegroom by the soul, has this for its subject.

Footnotes:

236. Matt. 10:33
237. Matt. 6:24
238. Phil. 1:21
239. Matt. 16:25
240. Cant. 6:2

A Spiritual Canticle of the Soul and the Bridegroom Christ

STANZA XXX

Of emeralds, and of flowers
In the early morning gathered,
We will make the garlands,
Flowering in Your love,
And bound together with one hair of my head.

THE bride now turns to the Bridegroom and addresses Him in the intercourse and comfort of love; the subject of the stanza being the solace and delight which the bride-soul and the Son of God find in the possession of the virtues and gifts of each other, and in the exercise thereof, both rejoicing in their mutual love. Thus the soul, addressing the Beloved, says that they will make garlands rich in graces and acquired virtues, obtained at the fitting and convenient season, beautiful and lovely in the love He bears the soul, and kept together by the love which it itself has for Him. This rejoicing in virtue is what is meant by making garlands, for the soul and God rejoice together in these virtues bound up as flowers in a garland, in the common love which each bears the other.

"Of emeralds, and of flowers."

2. The flowers are the virtues of the soul; the emeralds are the gifts it has received from God. Then of these flowers and emeralds

"In the early morning gathered."

3. That is, acquired in youth, which is the early morning of life. They are said to be gathered because the virtues which we acquire in youth are most pleasing to God; because youth is the season when our vices most resist the acquisition of them, and when our natural inclinations are most prone to lose them. Those virtues also are more perfect which we acquire in early youth. This time of our life is the early morning; for as the freshness of the spring morning is more agreeable than any other part of the day, so also are the virtues acquired in our youth more pleasing in the sight of God.

4. By the fresh morning we may understand those acts of love by which we acquire virtue, and which are more pleasing to God than the fresh morning is to the sons of men; good works also, wrought in the season of spiritual dryness and hardness; this is the freshness of the winter morning, and what we then do for God in dryness of spirit is most precious in His eyes. Then it is that we acquire virtues and graces abundantly; and what we then acquire with toil and labor is for the most part better, more perfect and lasting than what we acquire in comfort and spiritual sweetness; for virtue sends forth its roots in the season of dryness, toil, and trial: as it is written, "Virtue is made perfect in infirmity." [241] It is with a view to show forth the excellence of these virtues, of which the garland is wrought for the Beloved, that the soul says of them that they have been gathered in the early morning; because it is these flowers alone, with the emeralds of virtue, the choice and perfect graces, and not the imperfect, which are pleasing to the Beloved, and so the bride says:

"We will make the garlands."

5. All the virtues and graces which the soul, and God in it, acquire are as a garland of diverse flowers with which the soul is marvelously adorned as with a vesture of rich embroidery. As material flowers are gathered, and then formed into a garland, so the spiritual flowers of virtues and graces are acquired and set in order in the soul: and when the acquisition is complete, the garland of perfection is complete also. The soul and the Bridegroom rejoice in it, both beautiful, adorned with the garland, as in the state of perfection.

6. These are the garlands which the soul says they will make. That is, it will wreathe itself with this variety of flowers, with the emeralds of virtues and perfect gifts, that it may present itself worthily before the face of the King, and be on an equality with Him, sitting as a queen on His right hand; for it has merited this by its beauty. Thus David says, addressing himself to Christ: "The queen stood on Your

right hand in vestments of gold, girt with variety." [242] That is, at His right hand, clad in perfect love, girt with the variety of graces and perfect virtues.

7. The soul does not say, "I will make garlands," nor "You will make them," but, "We will make them," not separately, but both together; because the soul cannot practice virtues alone, nor acquire them alone, without the help of God; neither does God alone create virtue in the soul without the soul's concurrence. Though it is true, as the Apostle says, that "every best gift, and every perfect gift, is from above, descending from the Father of lights," [243] still they enter into no soul without that soul's concurrence and consent. Thus the bride in the Canticle says to the Bridegroom; "Draw me; we will run after you." [244] Every inclination to good comes from God alone, as we learn here; but as to running, that is, good works, they proceed from God and the soul together, and it is therefore written, "We will run" -- that is, both together, but not God nor the soul alone.

8. These words may also be fittingly applied to Christ and His Church, which, as His bride, says to Him, "We will make the garlands." In this application of the words the garlands are the holy souls born to Christ in the Church. Every such soul is by itself a garland adorned with the flowers of virtues and graces, and all of them together a garland for the head of Christ the Bridegroom.

9. We may also understand by these beautiful garlands the crowns formed by Christ and the Church, of which there are three kinds. The first is formed of the beauty and white flowers of the virgins, each one with her virginal crown, and forming altogether one crown for the head of the Bridegroom Christ. The second, of the brilliant flowers of the holy doctors, each with his crown of doctor, and all together forming one crown above that of the virgins on the head of Christ. The third is composed of the purple flowers of the martyrs, each with his own crown of martyrdom, and all united into one, perfecting that on the head of Christ. Adorned with these garlands He will be so beautiful, and so lovely to behold, that heaven itself will repeat the words of the bride in the Canticle, saying: "Go forth, you daughters of Zion, and see king Solomon in the diadem with which his mother crowned him in the day of his betrothal, and in the day of the joy of his heart." [245] The soul then says we will make garlands.

"Flowering in Your love."

10. The flowering of good works and virtues is the grace and power which they derive from the love of God, without which they not only flower not, but even become dry, and worthless in the eyes of God, though they may be humanly perfect. But if He gives His grace and love they flourish in His love.

"And bound together with one hair of my head."

11. The hair is the will of the soul, and the love it bears the Beloved. This love performs the function of the thread that keeps the garland together. For as a thread binds the flowers of a garland, so loves knits together and sustains virtues in the soul. "Charity" -- that is, love -- says the Apostle, "is the bond of perfection." [246] Love, in the same way, binds the virtues and supernatural gifts together, so that when love fails by our departure from God, all our virtue perishes also, just as the flowers drop from the garland when the thread that bound them together is broken. It is not enough for God's gift of virtues that He should love us, but we too must love Him in order to receive them, and preserve them.

12. The soul speaks of one hair, not of many, to show that the will by itself is fixed on God, detached from all other hairs; that is, from strange love. This points out the great price and worth of these garlands of virtues; for when love is single, firmly fixed on God, as here described, the virtues also are entire, perfect, and flowering in the love of God; for the love He bears the soul is beyond all price, and the soul also knows it well.

13. Were I to attempt a description of the beauty of that binding of the flowers and emeralds together, or of the strength and majesty which their harmonious arrangement furnishes to the soul, or the beauty and grace of its embroidered vesture, expressions and words would fail me; for if God says of the evil spirit, "His body is like molten shields, shut close up with scales pressing upon one another, one is joined to another, and not so much as any air can come between them"; [247] if the evil spirit is so strong, clad in malice thus compacted together -- for the scales that cover his body like molten shields are malice, and malice is in itself but weakness -- what must be the strength of the soul that is clothed in virtues so compacted and united together that no impurity or imperfection can penetrate between them; each virtue severally adding strength to strength, beauty to beauty, wealth to wealth, and to majesty, dominion and grandeur?

14. What a marvelous vision will be that of the bride-soul, when it shall sit on the right hand of the Bridegroom-King, crowned with graces! "How beautiful are your steps in shoes, O prince's daughter!"[248] The soul is called a prince's daughter because of the power it has; and if the beauty of the steps in shoes is great, what must be that of the whole vesture? Not only is the beauty of the soul crowned with admirable flowers, but its strength also, flowing from the harmonious order of the

A Spiritual Canticle of the Soul and the Bridegroom Christ

flowers, intertwined with the emeralds of its innumerable graces, is terrible: "Terrible as the army of a camp set in array." [249] For, as these virtues and gifts of God refresh the soul with their spiritual perfume, so also, when united in it, do they, out of their substance, minister strength. Thus, in the Canticle, when the bride was weak, languishing with love -- because she had not been able to bind together the flowers and the emeralds with the hair of her love -- and anxious to strengthen herself by that union of them, cries out: "Stay me with flowers, compass me about with apples; because I languish with love." [250] The flowers are the virtues, and the apples are the other graces.

NOTE

I BELIEVE I have now shown how the intertwining of the garlands and their lasting presence in the soul explain the divine union of love which now exists between the soul and God. The Bridegroom, as He says Himself, is the "flower of the field and the lily of the valleys," [251] and the soul's love is the hair that unites to itself this flower of flowers. Love is the most precious of all things, because it is the "bond of perfection," as the Apostle says, [252] and perfection is union with God. The soul is, as it were, a sheaf of garlands, for it is the subject of this glory, no longer what it was before, but the very perfect flower of flowers in the perfection and beauty of all; for the thread of love binds so closely God and the soul, and so unites them, that it transforms them and makes them one by love; so that, though in essence different, yet in glory and appearance the soul seems God and God the soul. Such is this marvelous union, baffling all description.

2. We may form some conception of it from the love of David and Jonathan, whose "soul was knit with the soul of David." [253] If the love of one man for another can be thus strong, so as to knit two souls together, what must that love of God be which can knit the soul of man to God the Bridegroom? God Himself is here the suitor Who in the omnipotence of His unfathomable love absorbs the soul with greater violence and efficacy than a torrent of fire a single drop of the morning dew which resolves itself into air. The hair, therefore, which accomplishes such a union must, of necessity, be most strong and subtle, seeing that it penetrates and binds together so effectually the soul and God. In the present stanza the soul declares the qualities of this hair.

Footnotes:

241. 2 Cor 12:9
242. Ps. 44:10
243. James 1:17
244. Cant. 1:3
245. Cant. 3:11
246. Col. 3:14
247. Job 41:6, 7
248. Cant. 7:1
249. Cant. 6:3
250. Cant. 2:5
251. Cant. 2:1
252. Col. 3:14
253. 1 Kings 18:1

St. John of the Cross

STANZA XXXI

*By that one hair
You have observed fluttering on my neck,
And on my neck regarded,
You were captivated;
And wounded by one of my eyes.*

THERE are three things mentioned here. The first is, that the love by which the virtues are bound together is nothing less than a strong love; for in truth it need be so in order to preserve them. The second is, that God is greatly taken by this hair of love, seeing it to be alone and strong. The third is, that God is deeply enamored of the soul, beholding the purity and integrity of its faith.

"By that one hair You have observed fluttering on my neck."

2. The neck signifies that strength in which, it is said, fluttered the hair of love, strong love, which bound the virtues together. It is not sufficient for the preservation of virtues that love be alone, it must be also strong so that no contrary vice may anywhere destroy the perfection of the garland; for the virtues so are bound up together in the soul by the hair, that if the thread is once broken, all the virtues are lost; for where one virtue is, all are, and where one fails, all fail also. The hair is said to flutter on the neck, because its love of God, without any hindrance whatever, flutters strongly and lightly in the strength of the soul.

3. As the air causes hair to wave and flutter on the neck, so the breath of the Holy Spirit stirs the strong love that it may fly upwards to God; for without this divine wind, which excites the powers of the soul to the practice of divine love, all the virtues the soul may possess become ineffectual and fruitless. The Beloved observed the hair fluttering on the neck -- that is, He considered it with particular attention and regard; because strong love is a great attraction for the eyes of God.

"And on my neck regarded."

4. This shows us that God not only esteems this love, seeing it alone, but also loves it, seeing it strong; for to say that God regards is to say that He loves, and to say that He observes is to say that He esteems what He observes. The word "neck" is repeated in this line, because it, being strong, is the cause why God loves it so much. It is as if the soul said, "You have loved it, seeing it strong without weakness or fear, and without any other love, and flying upwards swiftly and fervently."

5. Until now God had not looked upon this hair so as to be captivated by it, because He had not seen it alone, separate from the others, withdrawn from other loves, feelings, and affections, which hindered it from fluttering alone on the neck of strength. Afterwards, however, when mortifications and trials, temptations and penance had detached it, and made it strong, so that nothing whatever could break it, then God beholds it, and is taken by it, and binds the flowers of the garlands with it; for it is now so strong that it can keep the virtues united together in the soul.

6. But what these temptations and trials are, how they come, and how far they reach, that the soul may attain to that strength of love in which God unites it to Himself, I have described in the "Dark Night," [254] and in the explanation of the four stanzas [255] which begin with the words, "O living flame of love!" The soul having passed through these trials has reached a degree of love so high that it has merited the divine union.

"You were captivated."

7. O joyful wonder! God captive to a hair. The reason of this capture so precious is that God was pleased to observe the fluttering of the hair on the soul's neck; for where God regards He loves. If He in His grace and mercy had not first looked upon us and loved us, [256] as St. John says, and humbled Himself, He never could have been taken by the fluttering of the hair of our miserable love. His flight is not so low as that our love could lay hold of the divine bird, attract His attention, and fly so high with a

A Spiritual Canticle of the Soul and the Bridegroom Christ

strength worthy of His regard, if He had not first looked upon us. He, however, is taken by the fluttering of the hair; He makes it worthy and pleasing to Himself, and then is captivated by it. "You have seen it on my neck, You were captivated by it." This renders it credible that a bird which flies low may capture the royal eagle in its flight, if the eagle should fly so low and be taken by it willingly.

"And wounded by one of my eyes."

8. The eye is faith. The soul speaks of but one, and that this has wounded the Beloved. If the faith and trust of the soul in God were not one, without admixture of other considerations, God never could have been Wounded by love. Thus the eye that wounds, and the hair that binds, must be one. So strong is the love of the Bridegroom for the bride, because of her simple faith, that, if the hair of her love binds Him, the eye of her faith imprisons Him so closely as to wound Him through that most tender affection He bears her, which is to the bride a further progress in His love.

9. The Bridegroom Himself speaks in the Canticle of the hair and the eyes, saying to the bride, "You have wounded My heart, My sister, My bride; you have wounded My heart with one of your eyes, and with one hair of your neck." [257] He says twice that His heart is wounded, that is, with the eye and the hair, and therefore the soul in this stanza speaks of them both, because they signify its union with God in the understanding and the will; for the understanding is subdued by faith, signified by the eye, and the will by love. Here the soul exults in this union, and gives thanks to the Bridegroom for it, it being His gift; accounting it a great matter that He has been pleased to requite its love, and to become captive to it. We may also observe here the joy, happiness, and delight of the soul with its prisoner, having been for a long time His prisoner, enamored of Him.

NOTE

GREAT is the power and courage of love, for God is its prisoner. Blessed is the soul that loves, for it has made a captive of God Who obeys its good pleasure. Such is the nature of love that it makes those who love do what is asked of them, and, on the other hand, without love the utmost efforts will be fruitless, but one hair will bind those that love. The soul, knowing this, and conscious of blessings beyond its merits, in being raised up to so high a degree of love, through the rich endowments of graces and virtues, attributes all to the Beloved, saying:

Footnotes:

254. Dark Night,' Bk. 1, ch. 14.
255. Stanza ii. sect. 26 ff.
256. 1 John 4:10
257. Cant. 4:9

STANZA XXXII

When You regarded me,
Yours eyes imprinted in me Your grace:
For this You loved me again,
And thereby my eyes merited
To adore what in You they saw.

IT is the nature of perfect love to seek or accept nothing for itself, to attribute nothing to itself, but to refer all to the Beloved. If this is true of earthly love, how much more so of the love of God, the reason of which is so constraining. In the two foregoing stanzas the bride seemed to attribute something to herself; for she said that she would make garlands with her Beloved, and bind them with a hair of her head; that is a great work, and of no slight importance and worth: afterwards she said that she exulted in having captivated Him by a hair, and wounded Him with one of her eyes. All this seems as if she attributed great merits to herself. Now, however, she explains her meaning, and removes the wrong impression with great care and fear, lest any merit should be attributed to herself, and therefore less to God than His due, and less also than she desired. She now refers all to Him, and at the same time gives Him thanks, saying that the cause of His being the captive of the hair of her love, and of His being wounded by the eye of her faith, was His mercy in looking lovingly upon her, thereby rendering her lovely and pleasing in His sight; and that the loveliness and worth she received from Him merited His love, and made her worthy to adore her Beloved, and to bring forth good works worthy of His love and favor.

"When You regarded me."

2. That is, with loving affection, for I have already said, that where God regards there He loves.

"Yours eyes imprinted in me Your grace."

3. The eyes of the Bridegroom signify here His merciful divinity, which, mercifully inclined to the soul, imprints or infuses in it the love and grace by which He makes it beautiful, and so elevates it that He makes it the partaker of His divinity. When the soul sees to what height of dignity God has raised it, it says:

"For this You loved me again."

4. To love again is to love much; it is more than simple love, it is a twofold love, and for two reasons. Here the soul explains the two motives of the Bridegroom's love; He not only loved it because captivated by the hair, but He loved it again, because He was wounded with one of its eyes. The reason why He loved it so deeply is that He would, when He looked upon it, give it the grace to please Him, endowing it with the hair of love, and animating with His charity the faith of the eye. And therefore the soul says:

"For this You loved me again."

5. To say that God shows favor to the soul is to say that He renders it worthy and capable of His love. It is therefore as if the soul said, "Having shown Your favor to me, worthy pledges of Your love, You have therefore loved me again"; that is, "You have given me grace upon grace"; or, in the words of St. John, "grace for grace"; [258] grace for the grace He has given, that is more grace, for without grace we cannot merit His grace.

6. If we could clearly understand this truth, we must keep in mind that, as God loves nothing beside Himself, so loves He nothing more than Himself, because He loves all things with reference to Himself. Thus love is the final cause, and God loves nothing for what it is in itself. Consequently, when we say that God loves such a soul, we say, in effect, that He brings it in a manner to Himself, making it

A Spiritual Canticle of the Soul and the Bridegroom Christ

His equal, and thus it is He loves that soul in Himself with that very love with which He loves Himself. Every good work, therefore, of the soul in God is meritorious of God's love, because the soul in His favor, thus exalted, merits God Himself in every act.

"And thereby my eyes merited."

7. That is, "By the grace and favor which the eyes of Your compassion have wrought, when You looked upon me, rendering me pleasing in Your sight and worthy of Your regard."

"To adore what in You they saw."

8. That is: "The powers of my soul, O my Bridegroom, the eyes by which I can see You, although once fallen and miserable in the vileness of their mean occupations, have merited to look upon You." To look upon God is to do good works in His grace. Thus the powers of the soul merit in adoring because they adore in the grace of God, in which every act is meritorious. Enlightened and exalted by grace, they adored what in Him they saw, and what they saw not before, because of their blindness and meanness. What, then, have they now seen? The greatness of His power, His overflowing sweetness, infinite goodness, love, and compassion, innumerable benefits received at His hands, as well now when so near Him as before when far away. The eyes of the soul now merit to adore, and by adoring merit, for they are beautiful and pleasing to the Bridegroom. Before they were unworthy, not only to adore or behold Him, but even to look upon Him at all: great indeed is the stupidity and blindness of a soul without the grace of God.

9. It is a melancholy thing to see how far a soul departs from its duty when it is not enlightened by the love of God. For being bound to acknowledge these and other innumerable favors which it has every moment received at His hands, temporal as well as spiritual, and to worship and serve Him unceasingly with all its faculties, it not only does not do so, but is unworthy even to think of Him; nor does it make any account of Him whatever. Such is the misery of those who are living, or rather who are dead, in sin.

NOTE

FOR the better understanding of this and of what follows, we must keep in mind that the regard of God benefits the soul in four ways: it cleanses, adorns, enriches, and enlightens it, as the sun, when it shines, dries, warms, beautifies, and brightens the earth. When God has visited the soul in the three latter ways, whereby He renders it pleasing to Himself, He remembers its former uncleanness and sin no more: as it is written, "All the iniquities that he has wrought, I will not remember." [259]

God having once done away with our sin and uncleanness, He will look upon them no more; nor will He withhold His mercy because of them, for He never punishes twice for the same sin, according to the words of the prophet: "There shall not rise a double affliction." [260]

Still, though God forgets the sin He has once forgiven, we are not for that reason to forget it ourselves; for the Wise Man says, "Be not without fear about sin forgiven." [261] There are three reasons for this. We should always remember our sin, that we may not presume, that we may have a subject of perpetual thanksgiving, and because it serves to give us more confidence that we shall receive greater favors; for if, when we were in sin, God showed Himself to us so merciful and forgiving, how much greater mercies may we not hope for when we are clean from sin, and in His love?

The soul, therefore, calling to mind all the mercies it has received, and seeing itself united to the Bridegroom in such dignity, rejoices greatly with joy, thanksgiving, and love. In this it is helped exceedingly by the recollection of its former condition, which was so mean and filthy that it not only did not deserve that God should look upon it, but was unworthy that He should even utter its name, as He says by the mouth of the prophet David: "Nor will I be mindful of their names by My lips." [262] Thus the soul, seeing that there was, and that there can be, nothing in itself to attract the eyes of God, but that all comes from Him of pure grace and goodwill, attributes its misery to itself, and all the blessings it enjoys to the Beloved; and seeing further that because of these blessings it can merit now what it could not merit before, it becomes bold with God, and prays for the divine spiritual union, wherein its mercies are multiplied. This is the subject of the following stanza:

Footnotes:

258. John 1:16
259. Ezek. 18:22
260. Nahum 1:9
261. Ecclus. 5:5
262. Ps. 15:4

STANZA XXXIII

Despise me not,
For if I was swarthy once,
You can regard me now;
Since You have regarded me,
Grace and beauty have You given me.

THE soul now is becoming bold, and respects itself, because of the gifts and endowments which the Beloved has bestowed upon it. It recognizes that these things, while itself is worthless and underserving, are at least means of merit, and consequently it ventures to say to the Beloved, "Do not disregard me now, or despise me"; for if before it deserved contempt because of the filthiness of its sin, and the meanness of its nature, now that He has once looked upon it, and thereby adorned it with grace and beauty, He may well look upon it a second time and increase its grace and beauty. That He has once done so, when the soul did not deserved it, and had no attractions for Him, is reason enough why He should do so again and again.

"Despise me not."

2. The soul does not say this because it desires in any way to be esteemed -- for contempt and insult are of great price, and occasions of joy to the soul that truly loves God -- but because it acknowledges that in itself it merits nothing else, were it not for the gifts and graces it has received from God, as it appears from the words that follow.

"For if I was swarthy once."

3. "If, before You graciously looked upon me You found me in my filthiness, black with imperfections and sins, and naturally mean and vile,"

"You can regard me now; since You have regarded me."

4. After once looking upon me, and taking away my swarthy complexion, defiled by sin and disagreeable to look upon, when You rendered me lovely for the first time, You may well look upon me now -- that is, now I may be looked on and deserve to be regarded, and thereby to receive further favors at Your hands. For Your eyes, when they first looked upon me, not only took away my swarthy complexion, but rendered me also worthy of Your regard; for in Your look of love, --

"Grace and beauty have You given me."

5. The two preceding lines are a commentary on the words of St. John, "grace for grace," [263] for when God beholds a soul that is lovely in His eyes He is moved to bestow more grace upon it because He dwells well-pleased within it. Moses knew this, and prayed for further grace: he would, as it were, constrain God to grant it because he had already received so much "You have said: I know you by name, and you have found favor in My sight: if therefore I have found favor in Your sight, show me Your face, that I may know You, and may find grace before Yours eyes." [264]

6. Now a soul which in the eyes of God is thus exalted in grace, honorable and lovely, is for that reason an object of His unutterable love. If He loved that soul before it was in a state of grace, for His own sake, He loves it now, when in a state of grace, not only for His own sake, but also for itself. Thus enamored of its beauty, through its affections and good works, now that it is never without them, He bestows upon it continually further grace and love, and the more honorable and exalted He renders that soul, the more is He captivated by it, and the greater His love for it.

7. God Himself sets this truth before us, saying to His people, by the mouth of the prophet, "since you became honorable in My eyes, and glorious, I have loved you." [265] That is, "Since I have cast My eyes upon you, and thereby showed you favor, and made you glorious and honorable in My sight, you

A Spiritual Canticle of the Soul and the Bridegroom Christ

have merited other and further favors"; for to say that God loves, is to say that He multiplies His grace. The bride in the Canticle speaks to the same effect, saying, "I am black, but beautiful, O you daughters of Jerusalem." [266] and the Church adds, [267] saying, "Therefore has the King loved me, and brought me into His secret chamber." This is as much as saying: "O you souls who have no knowledge nor understanding of these favors, do not marvel that the heavenly King has shown such mercy to me as to plunge me in the depths of His love, for, though I am swarthy, He has so regarded me, after once looking upon me, that He could not be satisfied without betrothing me to Himself, and calling me into the inner chamber of His love."

8. Who can measure the greatness of the soul's exaltation when God is pleased with it? No language, no imagination is sufficient for this; for in truth God does this as God, to show that it is He who does it. The dealings of God with such a soul may in some degree be understood; but only in this way, namely, that He gives more to him who has more, and that His gifts are multiplied in proportion to the previous endowments of the soul. This is what He teaches us Himself in the Gospel, saying; "He that has to him shall be given, and he shall abound: but he that has not, from him shall be taken away even that which he has." [268]

9. Thus the talent of that servant, not then in favor with his lord, was taken from him and given to another who had gained others, so that the latter might have all, together with the favor of his lord. [269] God heaps the noblest and the greatest favors of His house, which is the Church militant as well as the Church triumphant, upon him who is most His friend, ordaining it thus for His greater honor and glory, as a great light absorbs many little lights. This is the spiritual sense of those words, already cited, [270] the prophet Isaiah addressed to the people of Israel: "I am the Lord your God, the Holy One of Israel, your Savior: I have given Egypt for your atonement and Seba for you. I will give men for you, and people for your life." [271]

10. Well may You then, O God, gaze upon and prize that soul which You regard, for You have made it precious by looking upon it, and given it graces which in Your sight are precious, and by which You are captivated. That soul, therefore, deserves that You should regard it not only once, but often, seeing that You have once looked upon it; for so is it written in the book of Esther by the Holy Spirit: "This honor is he worthy of, whom the king has a mind to honor." [272]

NOTE

THE gifts of love which the Bridegroom bestows on the soul in this state are inestimable; the praises and endearing expressions of divine love which pass so frequently between them are beyond all utterance. The soul is occupied in praising Him, and in giving Him thanks; and He in exalting, praising, and thanking the soul, as we see in the Canticle, where He thus speaks to the bride: "Behold, you are fair, O My love, behold, you are fair; your eyes are as those of doves." The bride replies: "Behold, you are fair, my Beloved, and comely." [273] These, and other like expressions, are addressed by them each to the other.

2. In the previous stanza the soul despised itself, and said it was swarthy and unclean, praising Him for His beauty and grace, Who, by looking upon the soul, rendered it gracious and beautiful. He, Whose way it is to exalt the humble, fixing His eyes upon the soul, as He was entreated to do, praises it in the following stanza. He does not call it swarthy, as the soul calls itself, but He addresses it as His white dove, praising it for its good dispositions, those of a dove and a turtle-dove.

Footnotes:

263. John 1:16
264. Exod. 33:12, 13
265. Isa. 43:4
266. Cant. 1:4
267. Antiphon in Vesper B. M. V.
268. Matt. 13:12
269. Matt. 25:28
270. Sect. 7.
271. Isa. 43:3
272. Esth. 6:11
273. Cant. 4:1, 6:3

St. John of the Cross

STANZA XXXIV

THE BRIDEGROOM

> The little white dove
> Has returned to the ark with the bough;
> And now the turtle-dove
> Its desired mate
> On the green banks has found.

IT is the Bridegroom Himself who now speaks. He celebrates the purity of the soul in its present state, the rich rewards it has gained, in having prepared itself, and labored to come to Him. He also speaks of its blessedness in having found the Bridegroom in this union, and of the fulfillment of all its desires, the delight and joy it has in Him now that all the trials of life and time are over.

"The little white dove."

2. He calls the soul, on account of its whiteness and purity -- effects of the grace it has received at the hands of God -- a dove, "the little white dove," for this is the term He applies to it in the Canticle, to mark its simplicity, its natural gentleness, and its loving contemplation. The dove is not only simple, and gentle without gall, but its eyes are also clear, full of love. The Bridegroom, therefore, to point out in it this character or loving contemplation, wherein it looks upon God, says of it that its eyes are those of a dove: "Your eyes are dove's eyes." [274]

"Has returned to the ark with the bough."

3. Here the Bridegroom compares the soul to the dove of Noah's ark, the going and returning of which is a figure of what befalls the soul. For as the dove went forth from the ark, and returned because it found no rest for its feet on account of the waters of the deluge, until the time when it returned with the olive branch in its mouth -- a sign of the mercy of God in drying the waters which had covered the earth -- so the soul went forth at its creation out of the ark of God's omnipotence, and having traversed the deluge of its sins and imperfections, and finding no rest for its desires, flew and returned on the air of the longings of its love to the ark of its Creator's bosom; but it only effected an entrance when God had dried the waters of its imperfections. Then it returned with the olive branch, that is, the victory over all things by His merciful compassion, to this blessed and perfect recollection in the bosom of the Beloved, not only triumphant over all its enemies, but also rewarded for its merits; for both the one and the other are symbolized by the olive bough. Thus the dove-soul returns to the ark of God not only white and pure as it went forth when He created it, but with the olive branch of reward and peace obtained by the conquest of itself.

"And now the turtle dove its desired mate on the green banks has found."

4. The Bridegroom calls the soul the turtle-dove, because when it is seeking after the Beloved it is like the turtle-dove when it cannot find its desired mate. It is said of the turtle-dove, when it cannot find its mate, that it will not sits on the green boughs, nor drink of the cool refreshing waters, nor retire to the shade, nor mingle with companions; but when it finds its mate then it does all this.

5. Such, too, is the condition of the soul, and necessarily, if it is to attain to union with the Bridegroom. The soul's love and anxiety must be such that it cannot rest on the green boughs of any joy, nor drink of the waters of this world's honor and glory, nor recreate itself with any temporal consolation, nor shelter itself in the shade of created help and protection: it must repose nowhere, it must avoid the society of all its inclinations, mourn in its loneliness, until it shall find the Bridegroom to its perfect contentment.

6. And because the soul, before it attained to this estate, sought the Beloved in great love, and was satisfied with nothing short of Him, the Bridegroom here speaks of the end of its labors, and the

A Spiritual Canticle of the Soul and the Bridegroom Christ

fulfillment of its desires, saying: "Now the turtle-dove its desired mate on the green banks has found." That is: Now the bride-soul sits on the green bough, rejoicing in her Beloved, drinks of the clear waters of the highest contemplation and of the wisdom of God; is refreshed by the consolations it finds in Him, and is also sheltered under the shadow of His favor and protection, which she had so earnestly desired. There is she deliciously and divinely comforted, refreshed and nourished, as she says in the, Canticle: "I sat down under His shadow Whom I desired, and His fruit was sweet to my palate." [275]

NOTE

THE Bridegroom proceeds to speak of the satisfaction which He derives from the happiness which the bride has found in that solitude wherein she desired to live -- a stable peace and unchangeable good. For when the bride is confirmed in the tranquillity of her soul and solitary love of the Bridegroom, she reposes so sweetly in the love of God, and God also in her, that she requires no other means or masters to guide her in the way of God; for God Himself is now her light and guide, fulfilling in her what He promised by the mouth of Hosea, saying: "I will lead her into the wilderness, and I will speak to her heart." [276] That is, it is in solitude that He communicates Himself, and unites Himself, to the soul, for to speak to the heart is to satisfy the heart, and no heart can be satisfied with less than God. And so the Bridegroom Says:

Footnotes:

274. Cant. 4:1
275. Cant. 2:3
276. Hos. 2:14

STANZA XXXV

In solitude she lived,
And in solitude built her nest;
And in solitude, alone
Has the Beloved guided her,
In solitude also wounded with love.

IN this stanza the Bridegroom is doing two things: one is, He is praising the solitude in which the soul once lived, for it was the means whereby it found the Beloved, and rejoiced in Him, away from all its former anxieties and troubles. For, as the soul abode in solitude, abandoning all created help and consolation, in order to obtain the fellowship and union of the Beloved, it deserved thereby possession of the peace of solitude in the Beloved, in Whom it reposes alone, undisturbed by any anxieties.

2. The second is this: the Bridegroom is saying that, inasmuch as the soul has desired to be alone, far away, for His sake, from all created things, He has been enamored of it because of its loneliness, has taken care of it, held it in His arms, fed it with all good things, and guided it to the deep things of God. He does not merely say that He is now the soul's guide, but that He is its only guide, without any intermediate help, either of angels or of men, either of forms or of figures; for the soul in this solitude has attained to true liberty of spirit, and is wholly detached from all subordinate means.

"In solitude she lived."

3. The turtle-dove, that is, the soul, lived in solitude before she found the Beloved in this state of union; for the soul that longs after God derives no consolation from any other companionship, -- yes, until it finds Him everything does but increase its solitude.

"And in solitude built her nest."

4. The previous solitude of the soul was its voluntary privation of all the comforts of this world, for the sake of the Bridegroom -- as in the instance of the turtledove -- its striving after perfection, and acquiring that perfect solitude wherein it attains to union with the Word, and in consequence to complete refreshment and repose. This is what is meant by "nest"; and the words of the stanza may be thus explained: "In that solitude, wherein the bride formerly lived, tried by afflictions and troubles, because she was not perfect, there, in that solitude, has she found refreshment and rest, because she has found perfect rest in God." This, too, is the spiritual sense of these words of the Psalmist: "The sparrow has found herself a house, and the turtle a nest for herself, where she may lay her young ones; [277] that is, a sure stay in God, in Whom all the desires and powers of the soul are satisfied."

"And in solitude."

5. In the solitude of perfect detachment from all things, wherein it lives alone with God -- there He guides it, moves it, and elevates it to divine things. He guides the understanding in the perception of divine things, because it is now detached from all strange and contrary knowledge, and is alone. He moves the will freely to love Himself, because it is now alone, disencumbered from all other affections. He fills the memory with divine knowledge, because that also is now alone, emptied of all imaginations and fancies. For the instant the soul clears and empties its faculties of all earthly objects, and from attachments to higher things, keeping them in solitude, God immediately fills them with the invisible and divine; it being God Himself Who guides it in this solitude. St. Paul says of the perfect, that they "are led by the Spirit of God," [278] and that is the same as saying "In solitude has He guided her."

"Alone has the Beloved guided her."

A Spiritual Canticle of the Soul and the Bridegroom Christ

6. That is, the Beloved not only guides the soul in its solitude, but it is He alone Who works in it directly and immediately. It is of the nature of the soul's union with God in the spiritual marriage that God works directly, and communicates Himself immediately, not by the ministry of angels or by the help of natural capacities. For the exterior and interior senses, all created things, and even the soul itself, contribute very little towards the reception of those great supernatural favors which God bestows in this state; indeed, inasmuch as they do not fall within the cognizance of natural efforts, ability and application, God effects them alone.

7. The reason is, that He finds the soul alone in its solitude, and therefore will not give it another companion, nor will He entrust His work to any other than Himself.

8. There is a certain fitness in this; for the soul having abandoned all things, and passed through all the ordinary means, rising above them to God, God Himself becomes the guide, and the way to Himself. The soul in solitude, detached from all things, having now ascended above all things, nothing now can profit or help it to ascend higher except the Bridegroom Word Himself, Who, because enamored of the bride, will Himself alone bestow these graces on the soul. And so He says:

"In solitude also wounded with love."

9. That is, the love of the bride; for the Bridegroom not only loves greatly the solitude of the soul, but is also wounded with love of her, because the soul would abide in solitude and detachment, on account of its being itself wounded with love of Him. He will not, therefore, leave it alone; for being wounded with love because of the soul's solitude on His account, and seeing that nothing else can satisfy it, He comes Himself to be alone its guide, drawing it to, and absorbing it in, Himself. But He would not have done so if He had not found it in this spiritual solitude.

NOTE

IT is a strange characteristic of persons in love that they take a much greater pleasure in their loneliness than in the company of others. For if they meet together in the presence of others with whom they need have no intercourse, and from whom they have nothing to conceal, and if those others neither address them nor interfere with them, yet the very fact of their presence is sufficient to rob the lovers of all pleasure in their meeting. The cause of this lies in the fact that love is the union of two persons, who will not communicate with each other if they are not alone. And now the soul, having reached the summit of perfection, and liberty of spirit in God, all the resistance and contradictions of the flesh being subdued, has no other occupation or employment than indulgence in the joys of its intimate love of the Bridegroom. It is written of holy Tobit, after the trials of his life were over, that God restored his sight, and that "the rest of his life was in joy." [279] So is it with the perfect soul, it rejoices in the blessings that surround it.

2. The prophet Isaiah says of the soul which, having been tried in the works of perfection has arrived at the goal desired: "Your light shall arise up in darkness, and your darkness shall be as the noonday. And the Lord will give you rest always, and will fill your soul with brightness, and deliver your bones, and you shall be as a watered garden and as a fountain of water whose waters shall not fail. And the deserts of the world shall be built in you: you shall raise up the foundations of generation and generation; and you shall be called the builder of the hedges, turning the paths into rest. If you turn away your foot from the Sabbath, from doing your will in My holy day, and call the Sabbath delicate, and the Holy of our Lord glorious, and glorify Him while you do not your own ways, and your will be not found, to speak a word: then shall you be delighted in the Lord, and I will lift you up above the heights of the earth, and will feed you with the inheritance of Jacob your father," [280] Who is God Himself. The soul, therefore, has nothing else to do now but to rejoice in the delights of this pasture, and one thing only to desire -- the perfect fruition of it in everlasting life. Thus, in the next and the following stanzas it implores the Beloved to admit it into this beatific pasture in the clear vision of God, and says:

Footnotes:

277. Ps. 83:4
278. Rom. 8:14
279. Tob. 14:4
280. Isa. 58:10-14

St. John of the Cross

STANZA XXXVI

THE BRIDE

> *Let us rejoice, O my Beloved,*
> *Let us go forth to see ourselves in Your beauty,*
> *To the mountain and the hill,*
> *Where the pure water flows:*
> *Let us enter into the heart of the thicket.*

THE perfect union of love between itself and God being now effected, the soul longs to occupy itself with those things that belong to love. It is the soul which is now speaking, making three petitions to the Beloved. In the first place, it asks for the joy and sweetness of love, saying, "Let us rejoice." In the second place, it prays to be made like Him, saying, "Let us go forth to see ourselves in Your beauty." In the third place, it begs to be admitted to the knowledge of His secrets, saying, "Let us enter into the heart of the thicket."

"Let us rejoice, O my Beloved."

2. That is, in the sweetness of our love; not only in that sweetness of ordinary union, but also in that which flows from active and affective love, whether in the will by an act of affection, or outwardly in good works which tend to the service of the Beloved. For love, as I have said, where it is firmly rooted, ever runs after those joys and delights which are the acts of exterior and interior love. All this the soul does that it may be made like to the Beloved.

"Let us go forth to see ourselves in Your beauty."

3. "Let us so act, that, by the practice of this love, we may come to see ourselves in Your beauty in everlasting life." That is: "Let me be so transformed in Your beauty, that, being alike in beauty, we may see ourselves both in Your beauty; having Your beauty, so that, one beholding the other, each may see his own beauty in the other, the beauty of both being Yours only, and mine absorbed in it. And thus I shall see You in Your beauty, and myself in Your beauty, and You shall see me in Your beauty; and I shall see myself in You in Your beauty, and You Yourself in me in Your beauty; so shall I seem to be Yourself in Your beauty, and You myself in Your beauty; my beauty shall be Yours, Yours shall be mine, and I shall be You in it, and You myself in Your own beauty; for Your beauty will be my beauty, and so we shall see, each the other, in Your beauty."

4. This is the adoption of the sons of God, who may truly say what the Son Himself says to the Eternal Father: "All My things are Yours, and Yours are Mine," [281] He by essence, being the Son of God by nature, we by participation, being sons by adoption. This He says not for Himself only, Who is the Head, but for the whole mystical body, which is the Church. For the Church will share in the very beauty of the Bridegroom in the day of her triumph, when she shall see God face to face. And this is the vision which the soul prays that the Bridegroom and itself may go in His beauty to see.

"To the mountain and the hill."

5. That is, to the morning and essential knowledge of God, [282] which is knowledge in the Divine Word, Who, because He is so high, is here signified by "the mountain." Thus Isaiah says, calling upon men to know the Son of God: "Come, and let us go up to the mountain of our Lord"; [283] and before: "In the last days the mountain of the house of the Lord shall be prepared." [284]

"And to the hill."

A Spiritual Canticle of the Soul and the Bridegroom Christ

6. That is, to the evening knowledge of God, to the knowledge of Him in His creatures, in His works, and in His marvelous laws. This is signified by the expression "hill," because it is a kind of knowledge lower than the other. The soul prays for both when it says "to the mountain and the hill."

7. When the soul says, "Let us go forth to see ourselves in Your beauty to the mountain," its meaning is, "Transform me, and make me like the beauty of the Divine Wisdom, the Word, the Son of God." When it says "to the hill," the meaning is, "Instruct me in the beauty of this lower knowledge, which is manifest in Your creatures and mysterious works." This also is the beauty of the Son of God, with which the soul desires to shine.

8. But the soul cannot see itself in the beauty of God if it is not transformed in His wisdom, wherein all things are seen and possessed, whether in heaven or in earth. It was to this mountain and to this hill the bride longed to come when she said, "I will go to the mountain of myrrh, and to the hill of frankincense." [285] The mountain of myrrh is the clear vision of God, and the hill of frankincense the knowledge of Him in His works, for the myrrh on the mountain is of a higher order than the incense on the hill.

"Where the pure water flows."

9. This is the wisdom and knowledge of God, which cleanse the understanding, and detach it from all accidents and fancies, and which clear it of the mist of ignorance. The soul is ever influenced by this desire of perfectly and clearly understanding the divine verities, and the more it loves the more it desires to penetrate them, and hence the third petition which it makes:

"Let us enter into the heart of the thicket;"

10. Into the depths of God's marvelous works and profound judgments. Such is their multitude and variety, that they may be called a thicket. They are so full of wisdom and mystery, that we may not only call them a thicket, but we may even apply to them the words of David: "The mountain of God is a rich mountain, a mountain curdled as cheese, a rich mountain." [286] The thicket of the wisdom and knowledge of God is so deep, and so immense, that the soul, however much it knows of it, can always penetrate further within it, because it is so immense and so incomprehensible. "O the depth," cries out the Apostle, "of the riches of the wisdom and of the knowledge of God! How incomprehensible are His judgments, and how unsearchable His ways!" [287]

11. But the soul longs to enter this thicket and incomprehensibility of His judgments, for it is moved by that longing for a deeper knowledge of them. That knowledge is an inestimable delight, transcending all understanding. David, speaking of the sweetness of them, says: "The judgments of our Lord are true, justified in themselves, to be desired above gold and many precious stones, and sweeter than honey and the honey-comb. For Your servant keeps them." [288] The soul therefore earnestly longs to be engulfed in His judgments, and to have a deeper knowledge of them, and for that end would esteem it a joy and great consolation to endure all sufferings and afflictions in the world, and whatever else might help it to that end, however hard and painful it might be; it would gladly pass through the agonies of death to enter deeper into God.

12. Hence, also, the thicket, which the soul desires to enter, may be fittingly understood as signifying the great and many trials and tribulations which the soul longs for, because suffering is most sweet and most profitable to it, inasmuch as it is the way by which it enters more and more into the thicket of the delicious wisdom of God. The most pure suffering leads to the most pure and the deepest knowledge, and consequently to the purest and highest joy, for that is the issue of the deepest knowledge. Thus, the soul, not satisfied with ordinary suffering, says, "Let us enter into the heart of the thicket," even the anguish of death, that I may see God.

13. Job, desiring to suffer that he might see God, thus speaks "Who will grant that my request may come, and that God may give me what I look for? And that He that has begun may destroy me, that He may let loose His hand and cut me off? And that this may be my comfort, that afflicting me with sorrow, He spare not." [289] O that men would understand how impossible it is to enter the thicket, the manifold riches of the wisdom of God, without entering into the thicket of manifold suffering making it the desire and consolation of the soul; and how that the soul which really longs for the divine wisdom longs first of all for the sufferings of the Cross, that it may enter in.

14. For this cause it was that St. Paul admonished the Ephesians not to faint in their tribulations, but to take courage: "That being rooted and founded in charity, you may be able to comprehend with all the saints what is the breadth, and length, and height, and depth; to know also the charity of Christ, which surpasses all knowledge, that you may be filled to all the fullness of God." [290] The gate by which we enter into the riches of the knowledge of God is the Cross; and that gate is narrow. They who desire to enter in that way are few, while those who desire the joys that come by it are many.

NOTE

ONE of the principal reasons why the soul desires to be released and to be with Christ is that it may see Him face to face, and penetrate to the depths of His ways and the eternal mysteries of His incarnation, which is not the least part of its blessedness; for in the Gospel of St. John He, addressing the Father, said: "Now this is eternal life: that they may know You, the only true God, and Jesus Christ Whom You have sent." [291] As the first act of a person who has taken a long journey is to see and converse with him whom he was in search of, so the first thing which the soul desires, when it has attained to the beatific vision, is to know and enjoy the deep secrets and mysteries of the incarnation and the ancient ways of God depending on them. Thus the soul, having said that it longed to see itself in the beauty of God, sings as in the following stanza:

Footnotes:

281. John 17:10
282. St. Augustine, De Genesi ad Litt.' iv., xxiv. (and elsewhere) and the scholastics (St. Thomas, S. Th.' I. lviii. 7) distinguish between the morning knowledge' whereby angels and saints know created things by seeing the Divine Word, and evening knowledge' where they derive their knowledge from the created things themselves.
283. Isa. 2:3
284. Isa. 2:2
285. Cant. 4:6
286. Ps. 67:16
287. Rom. 11:33
288. Ps. 18:10-12
289. Job 6:8-10
290. Eph. 3:17-19
291. John 17:3

A Spiritual Canticle of the Soul and the Bridegroom Christ

STANZA XXXVII

We shall go at once
To the deep caverns of the rock
Which are all secret;
There we shall enter in,
And taste of the new wine of the pomegranate.

ONE of the reasons which most influence the soul to desire to enter into the "thicket" of the wisdom of God, and to have a more intimate knowledge of the beauty of the divine wisdom, is, as I have said, that it may unite the understanding with God in the knowledge of the mysteries of the Incarnation, as of all His works the highest and most full of sweetness, and the most delicious knowledge. And here the bride therefore says, that after she has entered in within the divine wisdom -- that is, the spiritual marriage, which is now and will be in glory, seeing God face to face -- her soul united with the divine wisdom, the Son of God, she will then understand the deep mysteries of God and Man, which are the highest wisdom hidden in God. They, that is, the bride and the Bridegroom, will enter in -- the soul engulfed and absorbed -- and both together will have the fruition of the joy which springs from the knowledge of mysteries, and attributes and power of God which are revealed in those mysteries, such as His justice, His mercy, wisdom, power, and love.

"*We shall go at once to the deep caverns of the rock.*"

2. "This rock is Christ," as we learn from St. Paul. [292] The deep caverns of the rock are the deep mysteries of the wisdom of God in Christ, in the hypostatical union of the human nature with the Divine Word, and in the correspondence with it of the union of man with God, and in the agreement of God's justice and mercy in the salvation of mankind, in the manifestation of His judgments. And because His judgments are so high and so deep, they are here fittingly called "deep caverns"; deep because of the depth of His mysteries, and caverns because of the depth of His wisdom in them. For as caverns are deep, with many windings, so each mystery of Christ is of deepest wisdom, and has many windings of His secret judgments of predestination and foreknowledge with respect to men.

3. Notwithstanding the marvelous mysteries which holy doctors have discovered, and holy souls have understood in this life, many more remain behind. There are in Christ great depths to be fathomed, for He is a rich mine, with many recesses full of treasures, and however deeply we may descend we shall never reach the end, for in every recess new veins of new treasures abound in all directions: "In Whom," according to the Apostle, "are hid all the treasures of wisdom and knowledge." [293] But the soul cannot reach these hidden treasures unless it first passes through the thicket of interior and exterior suffering: for even such knowledge of the mysteries of Christ as is possible in this life cannot be had without great sufferings, and without many intellectual and moral gifts, and without previous spiritual exercises; for all these gifts are far inferior to this knowledge of the mysteries of Christ, being only a preparation for it.

4. Thus God said to Moses, when he asked to see His glory, "Man shall not see Me and live." God, however, said that He would show him all that could be revealed in this life; and so He set Moses "in a hole of the rock," which is Christ, where he might see His "back parts"; [294] that is, He made him understand the mysteries of the Sacred Humanity.

5. The soul longs to enter in earnest into these caverns of Christ, that it may be absorbed, transformed, and inebriated in the love and knowledge of His mysteries, hiding itself in the bosom of the Beloved. It is into these caverns that He invites the bride, in the Canticle, to enter, saying: "Arise, My love, My beautiful one, and come; My dove in the clefts of the rock, in the hollow places of the wall." [295] These clefts of the rock are the caverns of which we are here speaking, and to which the bride refers, saying:

"*And there we shall enter in.*"

6. That is, in the knowledge of the divine mysteries. The bride does not say "I will enter" alone, which seems the most fitting -- seeing that the Bridegroom has no need to enter in again -- but "we will enter," that is, the Bridegroom and the bride, to show that this is not the work of the bride, but of the Bridegroom with her. Moreover, inasmuch as God and the soul are now united in the state of spiritual marriage, the soul does nothing of itself without God. To say "we will enter," is as much as to say, "there shall we transform ourselves" -- that is, "I shall be transformed in You through the love of Your divine and sweet judgments": for in the knowledge of the predestination of the just and in the foresight of the wicked, wherein the Father prevented the just in the benedictions of His sweetness in Jesus Christ His Son, the soul is transformed in a most exalted and perfect way in the love of God according to this knowledge, giving thanks to the Father, and loving Him again and again with great sweetness and delight, for the sake of Jesus Christ His Son. This the soul does in union with Christ and together with Him. The delight flowing from this act of praise is ineffably sweet, and the soul speaks of it in the words that follow:

"And taste of the new wine of the pomegranates."

7. The pomegranates here are the mysteries of Christ and the judgments of the wisdom of God; His power and attributes, the knowledge of which we have from these mysteries; and they are infinite. For as pomegranates have many grains in their round orb, so in each one of the attributes and judgments and power of God is a multitude of admirable arrangements and marvelous works contained within the sphere of power and mystery, appertaining to those works. Consider the round form of the pomegranate; for each pomegranate signifies some one power and attribute of God, which power or attribute is God Himself, symbolized here by the circular figure, which has neither beginning not end. It was in the contemplation of the judgments and mysteries of the wisdom of God, which are infinite, that the bride said, "His belly is of ivory set with sapphires." [296] The sapphires are the mysteries and judgments of the divine Wisdom, which is here signified by the "belly" -- the sapphire being a precious stone of the color of the heavens when clear and serene.

8. The wine of the pomegranates which the bride says that she and the Bridegroom will taste is the fruition and joy of the love of God which overflows the soul in the understanding and knowledge of His mysteries. For as the many grains of the pomegranate pressed together give forth but one wine, so all the marvels and magnificence of God, infused into the soul, issue in but one fruition and joy of love, which is the drink of the Holy Spirit, and which the soul offers at once to God the Word, its Bridegroom, with great tenderness of love.

9. This divine drink the bride promised to the Bridegroom if He would lead her into this deep knowledge: "There You shall teach me," says the bride, "and I will give You a cup of spiced wine, and new wine of my pomegranates." [297] The soul calls them "my pomegranates," though they are God's Who had given them to it, and the soul offers them to God as if they were its own, saying, "We will taste of the wine of the pomegranates"; for when He states it He gives it to the soul to taste, and when the soul tastes it, the soul gives it back to Him, and thus it is that both taste it together.

NOTE

IN the two previous stanzas the bride sung of those good things which the Bridegroom is to give her in everlasting bliss, namely, her transformation in the beauty of created and uncreated wisdom, and also in the beauty of the union of the Word with flesh, wherein she shall behold His face as well as His back. Accordingly two things are set before us in the following stanza. The first is the way in which the soul tastes of the divine wine of the pomegranates; the second is the soul's putting before the Bridegroom the glory of its predestination. And though these two things are spoken of separately, one after the other, they are both involved in the one essential glory of the soul.

Footnotes:

292. 1 Cor. 10:4
293. Col. 2:3
294. Exod. 33:20-23
295. Cant. 2:13, 14
296. Cant. 5:14
297. Cant. 8:2

STANZA XXXVIII

There you will show me
That which my soul desired;
And there You will give at once,
O You, my life,
That which You gave me the other day.

THE reason why the soul longed to enter the caverns was that it might attain to the consummation of the love of God, the object of its continual desires; that is, that it might love God with the pureness and perfection with which He has loved it, so that it might thereby requite His love. Hence in the present stanza the bride says to the Bridegroom that He will there show her what she had always aimed at in all her actions, namely, that He would show her how to love Him perfectly, as He has loved her. And, secondly, that He will give her that essential glory for which He has predestined her from the day of His eternity.

"There You will show me That which my soul desired."

2. That which the soul aims at is equality in love with God, the object of its natural and supernatural desire. He who loves cannot be satisfied if he does not feel that he loves as much as he is loved. And when the soul sees that in the transformation in God, such as is possible in this life, notwithstanding the immensity of its love, it cannot equal the perfection of that love with which God loves it, it desires the clear transformation of glory in which it shall equal the perfection of love with which it is itself beloved of God; it desires, I say, the clear transformation of glory in which it shall equal His love.

3. For though in this high state, which the soul reaches on earth, there is a real union of the will, yet it cannot reach that perfection and strength of love which it will possess in the union of glory; seeing that then, according to the Apostle, the soul will know God as it is known of Him: "Then I shall know even as I am known." [298] That is, "I shall then love God even as I am loved by Him." For as the understanding of the soul will then be the understanding of God, and its will the will of God, so its love will also be His love. Though in heaven the will of the soul is not destroyed, it is so intimately united with the power of the will of God, Who loves it, that it loves Him as strongly and as perfectly as it is loved of Him; both wills being united in one sole will and one sole love of God.

4. Thus the soul loves God with the will and strength of God Himself, being made one with that very strength of love with which itself is loved of God. This strength is of the Holy Spirit, in Whom the soul is there transformed. He is given to the soul to strengthen its love; ministering to it, and supplying in it, because of its transformation in glory, that which is defective in it. In the perfect transformation, also, of the state of spiritual marriage, such as is possible on earth, in which the soul is all clothed in grace, the soul loves in a certain way in the Holy Spirit, Who is given to it in that transformation.

5. We are to observe here that the bride does not say, "There will You give me Your love," though that is true -- for that means only that God will love her -- but that He will there show her how she is to love Him with that perfection at which she aims, because there in giving her His love He will at the same time show her how to love Him as He loves her. For God not only teaches the soul to love Himself purely, with a disinterested love, as He has loved us, but He also enables it to love Him with that strength with which He loves the soul, transforming it in His love, wherein He bestows upon it His own power, so that it may love Him. It is as if He put an instrument in its hand, taught it the use thereof, and played upon it together with the soul. This is showing the soul how it is to love, and at the same time endowing it with the capacity of loving.

6. The soul is not satisfied until it reaches this point, neither would it be satisfied even in heaven, unless it felt, as St. Thomas teaches, [299] that it loved God as much as it is loved of Him. And as I said of the state of spiritual marriage of which I am speaking, there is now at this time, though it cannot be that perfect love in glory, a certain vivid vision and likeness of that perfection, which is wholly indescribable.

St. John of the Cross
"And there You will give me at once, O You my life, that which You gave me the other day."

7. What He will give is the essential glory which consists in the vision of God. Before proceeding further it is requisite to solve a question which arises here, namely, Why is it, seeing that essential glory consists in the vision of God, and not in loving Him, the soul says that its longing is for His love, and not for the essential glory? Why is it that the soul begins the stanza with referring to His love, and then introduces the subject of the essential glory afterwards, as if it were something of less importance?

8. There are two reasons for this. The first is this: As the whole aim of the soul is love, the seat of which is in the will, the property of which is to give and not to receive -- the property of the understanding, the subject of essential glory, being to receive and not to give -- to the soul inebriated with love the first consideration is not the essential glory which God will bestow upon it, but the entire surrender of itself to Him in true love, without any regard to its own advantage.

9. The second reason is that the second object is included in the first, and has been taken for granted in the previous stanzas, it being impossible to attain to the perfect love of God without the perfect vision of Him. The question is solved by the first reason, for the soul renders to God by love that which is His due, but with the understanding it receives from Him and does not give.

10. I now resume the explanation of the stanza, and inquire what day is meant by the "other day," and what is it that God then gave the soul, and what that is which it prays to receive afterwards in glory? By "other day" is meant the day of the eternity of God, which is other than the day of time. In that day of eternity God predestined the soul to glory, and determined the degree of glory which He would give it and freely gave from the beginning before He created it. This now, in a manner, so truly belongs to the soul that no event or accident, high or low, can ever take it away, for the soul will enjoy for ever that for which God had predestined it from all eternity.

11. This is that which He gave it "the other day"; that which the soul longs now to possess visibly in glory. And what is that which He gave it? That what "eye has not seen nor ear has heard, neither has it ascended into the heart of man." [300] "The eye has not seen," says Isaiah, "O God, beside You, what things You have prepared for them that expect You." [301] The soul has no word to describe it, so it says "what." It is in truth the vision of God, and as there is no expression by which we can explain what it is to see God, the soul says only "that which You gave me."

12. But that I may not leave the subject without saying something further concerning it, I will repeat what Christ has said of it in the Revelation of St. John, in many terms, phrases, and comparisons, because a single word once uttered cannot describe it, for there is much still unsaid, notwithstanding all that Christ has spoken at seven different times. "To him that overcomes," says He, "I will give to eat of the tree of life, which is in the paradise of My God." [302] But as this does not perfectly describe it, He says again: "Be faithful to death; and I will give you the crown of life." [303]

13. This also is insufficient, and so He speaks again more obscurely, but explaining it more: "To him that overcomes I will give the hidden manna, and will give him a white counter, and on the counter a new name written which no man knows but he that receives it." [304] And as even this is still insufficient, the Son of God speaks of great power and joy, saying: "He that shall overcome and keep My works to the end, I will give him power over the nations: and he shall rule them with a rod of iron, and as a vessel of the potter they shall be broken: as I also have received of My Father. And I will give him the morning star." [305] Not satisfied with these words, He adds: "He that shall overcome shall thus be vested in white garments, and I will not put his name out of the book of life, and I will confess his name before My Father." [306]

14. Still, all this falls short. He speaks of it in words of unutterable majesty and grandeur: "He that shall overcome I will make Him a pillar in the temple of My God, and he shall go out no more; and I will write upon him the name of My God, and the name of the city of My God, the new Jerusalem which descends out of heaven from My God, and My new name." [307] The seventh time He says: "He that shall overcome I will give to him to sit with Me in My throne: as I also have overcome, and sat with My Father in His throne. He that has an ear let him hear what the Spirit says to the Churches." [308]

15. These are the words of the Son of God; all of which tend to describe that which was given to the soul. The words correspond most accurately with it, but still they do not explain it, because it involves infinite good. The noblest expressions befit it, but none of them reach it, no, not all together.

16. Let us now see whether David has said anything of it. In one of the Psalms he says, "O how great is the multitude of your sweetness, O Lord, which You have hidden for them that fear You." [309] In another place he calls it a "torrent of pleasure," saying, "You shall make them drink of the torrent of Your pleasure." [310] And as he did not consider this enough, he says again, "You have prevented him with blessings of sweetness." [311] The expression that rightly fits this "that" of the soul, namely, its predestined bliss, cannot be found. Let us, therefore, rest satisfied with what the soul has used in reference to it, and explain the words as follows:

A Spiritual Canticle of the Soul and the Bridegroom Christ
"That which You gave me."

17. That is, "That weight of glory to which You predestined me, O my Bridegroom, in the day of Your eternity, when it was Your good pleasure to decree my creation, You will then give me in my day of my betrothal and of my nuptials, in my day of the joy of my heart, when, released from the burden of the flesh, led into the deep caverns of Your bridal chamber and gloriously transformed in You, we drink the wine of the sweet pomegranates."

NOTE

BUT inasmuch as the soul, in the state of spiritual marriage, of which I am now speaking, cannot but know something of this "that," seeing that because of its transformation in God something of it must be experienced by it, it will not omit to say something on the subject, the pledges and signs of which it is conscious of in itself, as it is written: "Who can withhold the words He has conceived?" [312] Hence in the following stanza the soul says something of the fruition which it shall have in the beatific vision, explaining so far as it is possible the nature and the manner of it.

Footnotes:

298. 1 Cor. 13:12
299. Opusc de Beatitudine,' ch. 2.
300. 1 Cor. 2:9
301. Isa. 64:4
302. Rev. 2:7
303. Rev. 2:10
304. Rev. 2:17
305. Rev. 2:26-28
306. Rev. 3:5
307. Rev. 3:12
308. Rev. 3:21,22
309. Ps. 30:20
310. Ps. 35:9
311. Ps. 20:4
312. Job 4:2

STANZA XXXIX

The breathing of the air,
The song of the sweet nightingale,
The grove and its beauty
In the serene night,
With the flame that consumes, and gives no pain.

THE soul refers here, under five different expressions, to that which the Bridegroom is to give it in the beatific transformation. 1. The aspiration of the Holy Spirit of God after it, and its own aspiration after God. 2. Joyous praise of God in the fruition of Him. 3. The knowledge of creatures and the order of them. 4. The pure and clear contemplation of the divine essence. 5. Perfect transformation in the infinite love of God.

"The breathing of the air."

2. This is a certain faculty which God will there give the soul in the communication of the Holy Spirit, Who, like one breathing, raises the soul by His divine aspiration, informs it, strengthens it, so that it too may breathe in God with the same aspiration of love which the Father breathes with the Son, and the Son with the Father, which is the Holy Spirit Himself, Who is breathed into the soul in the Father and the Son in that transformation so as to unite it to Himself; for the transformation will not be true and perfect if the soul is not transformed in the Three Persons of the Most Holy Trinity in a clear manifest degree. This breathing of the Holy Spirit in the soul, whereby God transforms it in Himself, is to the soul a joy so deep, so exquisite, and so grand that no mortal tongue can describe it, no human understanding, as such, conceive it in any degree; for even that which passes in the soul with respect to the communication which takes place in its transformation wrought in this life cannot be described, because the soul united with God and transformed in Him breathes in God that very divine aspiration which God breathes Himself in the soul when it is transformed in Him.

3. In the transformation which takes place in this life, this breathing of God in the soul, and of the soul in God, is of most frequent occurrence, and the source of the most exquisite delight of love to the soul, but not however in the clear and manifest degree which it will have in the life to come. This, in my opinion, is what St. Paul referred to when he said: "Because you are sons, God has sent the Spirit of His Son into your hearts, crying Abba, Father." [313] The blessed in the life to come, and the perfect in this, thus experience it.

4. Nor is it to be thought possible that the soul should be capable of so great a thing as that it should breathe in God as God in it, in the way of participation. For granting that God has bestowed upon it so great a favor as to unite it to the most Holy Trinity, whereby it becomes like God, and God by participation, is it altogether incredible that it should exercise the faculties of its understanding, perform its acts of knowledge and of love, or, to speak more accurately, should have it all done in the Holy Trinity together with It, as the Holy Trinity itself? This, however, takes place by communication and participation, God Himself effecting it in the soul, for this is "to be transformed in the Three Persons" in power, wisdom, and love, and herein it is that the soul becomes like God, Who, that it might come to this, created it to His own image and likeness.

5. How this can be so cannot be explained in any other way than by showing how the Son of God has raised us to so high a state, and merited for us the "power to be made the sons of God." [314] He prayed to the Father, saying: "Father, I will that where I am they also whom You have given Me may be with Me, that they may see My glory which You have given Me." [315] That is, "that they may do by participation in Us what I do naturally, namely, breathe the Holy Spirit." He says also: "Not for them only do I pray, but for them also who through their word shall believe in Me; that they all may be one, as You, Father, in Me, and I in You, that they also may be one in Us: that the world may believe that You have sent Me. And the glory which You have given Me, I have given to them: that they may be one as We also are one. I in them and You in Me, that they may be made perfect in one, and the world may know that You have sent Me, and have loved them as You have also loved Me," [316] -- that is, in bestowing upon them that love which He bestows upon the Son, though not naturally as upon Him, but

A Spiritual Canticle of the Soul and the Bridegroom Christ

in the way I speak of, in the union and transformation of love.

6. We are not to suppose from this that our Lord prayed that the saints might become one in essence and nature, as the Father and the Son are; but that they might become one in the union of love as the Father and the Son are one in the oneness of love. Souls have by participation that very God which the Son has by nature, and are therefore really gods by participation like unto God and of His society.

7. St. Peter speaks of this as follows: "Grace to you and peace be accomplished in the knowledge of God, and Christ Jesus our Lord; as all things of His divine power, which pertain to life and godliness, are given us by the knowledge of Him Who has called us by His own proper glory and virtue, by Whom He has given us most great and precious promises: that by these you may be made partakers of the divine nature." [317] Thus far St. Peter, who clearly teaches that the soul will be a partaker of God Himself, and will do, together with Him, the work of the Most Holy Trinity, because of the substantial union between the soul and God. And though this union is perfect only in the life to come, yet even in this, in the state of perfection, which the soul is said now to have attained, some anticipation of its sweetness is given it, in the way I am speaking of, though in a manner wholly ineffable.

8. O souls created for this and called to this, what are you doing? What are your occupations? Your aim is meanness, and your enjoyments misery. Oh, wretched blindness of the children of Adam, blind to so great a light, and deaf to so clear a voice; you do not see that, while seeking after greatness and glory, you are miserable and contemptible, ignorant, and unworthy of blessings so great. I now proceed to the second expression which the soul has made use of to describe that which He gave it.

"The song of the sweet nightingale."

9. Out of this "breathing of the air" comes the sweet voice of the Beloved addressing Himself to the soul, in which the soul sends forth its own sweet song of joy to Him. Both are meant by the song of the nightingale. As the song of the nightingale is heard in the spring of the year, when the cold, and rain, and changes of winter are past, filling the ear with melody, and the mind with joy; so, in the true intercourse and transformation of love, which takes place in this life, the bride, now protected and delivered from all trials and changes of the world, detached, and free from the imperfections, sufferings, and darkness both of mind and body, becomes conscious of a new spring in liberty, largeness, and joy of spirit, in which she hears the sweet voice of the Bridegroom, Who is her sweet nightingale, renewing and refreshing the very substance of her soul, now prepared for the journey of everlasting life.

10. That voice is sweet to her ears, and calls her sweetly, as it is written: "Arise, make haste, My love, My dove, My beautiful one, and come. For winter is now past, the rain is over and gone. The flowers have appeared in our land, the time of pruning is come: the voice of the turtle is heard in our land." [318] When the bride hears the voice of the Bridegroom in her inmost soul, she feels that her troubles are over and her prosperity begun. In the refreshing comfort and sweet sense of this voice she, too, like the nightingale, sends forth a new song of rejoicing to God, in unison with Him Who now moves her to do so.

11. It is for this that the Beloved sings, that the bride in unison with Him may sing to God; this is the aim and desire of the Bridegroom, that the soul should sing with the spirit joyously to God; and this is what He asks of the bride in the Canticle: "Arise, my love, my beautiful one, and come; my dove in the clefts of the rock, in the hollow places of the wall, show me your face, let your voice sound in my ears." [319]

12. The ears of God signify the desire He has that the soul should sing in perfect joy. And that this song may be perfect, the Bridegroom bids the soul to send it forth, and to let it sound in the clefts of the rock, that is, in the transformation which is the fruit of the mysteries of Christ, of which I spoke just now. [320] And because in this union of the soul with God, the soul sings to Him together with Him, in the way I spoke of when I was speaking of love, [321] the song of praise is most perfect and pleasing to God; for the acts of the soul, in the state of perfection, are most perfect; and thus the song of its rejoicing is sweet to God as well as to itself.

13. "Your voice is sweet," [322] says the Bridegroom, "not only to you, but also to Me, for as we are one, your voice is also in unison and one with Mine." This is the Canticle which the soul sings in the transformation which takes place in this life, about which no exaggeration is possible. But as this song is not so perfect as the new song in the life of glory, the soul, having a foretaste of that by what it feels on earth, shadows forth by the grandeur of this the magnificence of that in glory, which is beyond all comparison nobler, and calls it to mind and says that what its portion there will be is the song of the sweet nightingale.

"The grove and its beauty."

14. This is the third thing which the Bridegroom is to give the soul. The grove, because it contains many plants and animals, signifies God as the Creator and Giver of life to all creatures, which have their being and origin from Him, reveal Him and make Him known as the Creator. The beauty of the grove, which the soul prays for, is not only the grace, wisdom, and loveliness which flow from God over all created things, whether in heaven or on earth, but also the beauty of the mutual harmony and wise arrangement of the inferior creation, and the higher also, and of the mutual relations of both. The knowledge of this gives the soul great joy and delight. The fourth request is:

"In the serene night."

15. That is, contemplation, in which the soul desires to behold the grove. It is called night, because contemplation is dim; and that is the reason why it is also called mystical theology -- that is, the secret or hidden wisdom of God, where, without the sound of words, or the intervention of any bodily or spiritual sense, as it were in silence and in repose, in the darkness of sense and nature, God teaches the soul -- and the soul knows not how -- in a most secret and hidden way.

16. Some spiritual writers call this "understanding without understanding," because it does not take place in what philosophers call the active understanding which is conversant with the forms, fancies, and apprehensions of the physical faculties, but in the understanding as it is possible and passive, which without receiving such forms receives passively only the substantial knowledge of them free from all imagery. This occurs without effort or exertion on its part, and for this reason contemplation is called night, in which the soul through the channel of its transformation learns in this life that it already possesses, in a supreme degree, this divine grove, together with its beauty.

17. Still, however clear may be its knowledge, it is dark night in comparison with that of the blessed, for which the soul prays. Hence, while it prays for the clear contemplation, that is, the fruition of the grove, and its beauty; with the other objects here enumerated, it says, let it be in the night now serene; that is, in the clear beatific contemplation: let the night of dim contemplation cease here below, and change into the clear contemplation of the serene vision of God above. Thus the serene night is the clear and unclouded contemplation of the face of God. It was to this night of contemplation that David referred when he said, "Night shall be my light in my pleasures"; [323] that is, when I shall have my delight in the essential vision of God, the night of contemplation will have dawned in the day and light of my understanding.

"With the flame that consumes, and gives no pain."

18. This flame is the love of the Holy Spirit. "Consumes" means absolute perfection. Therefore, when the soul says that the Beloved will give it all that is mentioned in this stanza, and that they will be its possession in love absolute and perfect, all of them and itself with them in perfect love, and that without pain, its purpose is to show forth the utter perfection of love. Love, to be perfect, must have these two properties: it must consume and transform the soul in God; the burning and transformation wrought in the soul by the flame must give no pain. But this can be only in the state of the blessed, where the flame is sweet love, for in this transformation of the soul therein there is a blessed agreement and contentment on both sides, and no change to a greater or less degree gives pain, as before, when the soul had attained to the state of perfect love.

19. But the soul having attained to this state abides in its love of God, a love so like His and so sweet, God being, as Moses says, [324] a consuming fire -- "the Lord your God is a consuming fire" -- that it perfects and renews it. But this transformation is not like that which is wrought in this life, which though most perfect and in love consummate was still in some measure consuming the soul and wearing it away. It was like fire in burning coals, for though the coals may be transformed into fire, and made like it, and ceased from seething, and smoke no longer arises from them as before they were wholly transformed into fire, still, though they have become perfect fire, the fire consumes them and reduces them to ashes.

20. So is it with the soul which in this life is transformed by perfect love: for though it is wholly conformed, yet it still suffers, in some measure, both pain and loss. Pain, on account of the beatific transformation which is still wanting; loss, through the weakness and corruption of the flesh coming in contact with love so strong and so deep; for everything that is grand hurts and pains our natural infirmity, as it is written, "The corruptible body is a load upon the soul." [325] But in the life of bliss there will be neither loss nor pain, though the sense of the soul will be most acute, and its love without measure, for God will give power to the former and strength to the latter, perfecting the understanding in His wisdom and the will in His love.

21. As, in the foregoing stanzas, and in the one which follows, the bride prays for the boundless knowledge of God, for which she requires the strongest and the deepest love that she may love Him in proportion to the grandeur of His communications, she prays now that all these things may be bestowed

A Spiritual Canticle of the Soul and the Bridegroom Christ
upon her in love consummated, perfect, and strong.

Footnotes:

313. Gal. 4:6
314. John 1:12
315. John 17:24
316. John 17:20-23
317. 2 Pet. 1:2-4
318. Cant. 2:10-12
319. Cant. 2:13, 14
320. Stanza xxxvii. sect. 5.
321. Stanza xxxviii. sect. 6.
322. Cant. 2:14
323. Ps. 138:11
324. Deut. 4:24
325. Wisd. 9:15

STANZA XL

None saw it;
Neither did Aminadab appear
The siege was intermitted,
And the cavalry dismounted
At the sight of the waters.

THE bride perceiving that the desire of her will is now detached from all things, cleaving to God with most fervent love; that the sensual part of the soul, with all its powers, faculties, and desires, is now conformed to the spirit; that all rebellion is quelled forever; that Satan is overcome and driven far away in the varied contest of the spiritual struggle; that her soul is united and transformed in the rich abundance of the heavenly gifts; and that she herself is now prepared, strong and apparelled, "leaning upon her Beloved," to go up "by the desert" [326] of death; full of joy to the glorious throne of her espousals, -- she is longing for the end, and puts before the eyes of her Bridegroom, in order to influence Him the more, all that is mentioned in the present stanza, these five considerations:

2. The first is that the soul is detached from all things and a stranger to them. The second is that the devil is overcome and put to flight. The third is that the passions are subdued, and the natural desires mortified. The fourth and the fifth are that the sensual and lower nature of the soul is changed and purified, and so conformed to the spiritual, as not only not to hinder spiritual blessings, but is, on the contrary, prepared for them, for it is even a partaker already, according to its capacity, of those which have been bestowed upon it.

"None saw it."

3. That is, my soul is so detached, so denuded, so lonely, so estranged from all created things, in heaven and earth; it has become so recollected in You, that nothing whatever can come within sight of that most intimate joy which I have in You. That is, there is nothing whatever that can cause me pleasure with its sweetness, or disgust with its vileness; for my soul is so far removed from all such things, absorbed in such profound delight in You, that nothing can behold me. This is not all, for:

"Neither did Aminadab appear."

4. Aminadab, in the Holy Writings, signifies the devil; that is the enemy of the soul, in a spiritual sense, who is ever fighting against it, and disturbing it with his innumerable artillery, that it may not enter into the fortress and secret place of interior recollection with the Bridegroom. There, the soul is so protected, so strong, so triumphant in virtue which it then practices, so defended by God's right hand, that the devil not only dares not approach it, but runs away from it in great fear, and does not venture to appear. The practice of virtue, and the state of perfection to which the soul has come, is a victory over Satan, and causes him such terror that he cannot present himself before it. Thus Aminadab did not appear with any right to keep the soul away from the object of its desire.

"The siege was intermitted."

5. By the siege is meant the passions and desires, which, when not overcome and mortified, surround the soul and fight against it on all sides. Hence the term "siege" is applied to them. This siege is "intermitted" -- that is, the passions are subject to reason and the desires mortified. Under these circumstances the soul entreats the Beloved to communicate to it those graces for which it has prayed, for now the siege is no hindrance. Until the four passions of the soul are ordered in reason according to God, and until the desires are mortified and purified, the soul is incapable of seeing God.

"The cavalry dismounted at the sight of the waters."

A Spiritual Canticle of the Soul and the Bridegroom Christ

6. The waters are the spiritual joys and blessings which the soul now enjoys interiorly with God. The cavalry is the bodily senses of the sensual part, interior as well as exterior, for they carry with them the phantasms and figures of their objects. They dismount now at the sight of the waters, because the sensual and lower part of the soul in the state of spiritual marriage is purified, and in a certain way spiritualized, so that the soul with its powers of sense and natural forces becomes so recollected as to participate and rejoice, in their way, in the spiritual grandeurs which God communicates to it in the spirit within. To this the Psalmist referred when he said, "My heart and my flesh have rejoiced in the living God." [327]

7. It is to be observed that the cavalry did not dismount to taste of the waters, but only at the sight of them, because the sensual part of the soul, with its powers, is incapable of tasting substantially and properly the spiritual blessings, not merely in this life, but also in the life to come. Still, because of a certain overflowing of the spirit, they are sensibly refreshed and delighted, and this delight attracts them -- that is, the senses with their bodily powers -- towards that interior recollection where the soul is drinking the waters of the spiritual benedictions. This condition of the senses is rather a dismounting at the sight of the waters than a dismounting for the purpose of seeing or tasting them. The soul says of them that they dismounted, not that they went, or did anything else, and the meaning is that in the communication of the sensual with the spiritual part of the soul, when the spiritual waters become its drink, the natural operations subside and merge into spiritual recollection.

8. All these perfections and dispositions of the soul the bride sets forth before her Beloved, the Son of God, longing at the same time to be translated by Him out of the spiritual marriage, to which God has been pleased to advance her in the Church militant, to the glorious marriage of the Church triumphant. To that end may He bring of His mercy all those who call upon the most sweet name of Jesus, the Bridegroom of faithful souls, to Whom be all honor and glory, together with the Father and the Holy Spirit,

IN SÆCULA SÆCULORUM.

Footnotes:

326. Cant. 3:6; 8:5
327. Ps. 83:3

CPSIA information can be obtained
at www.ICGtesting.com
Printed in the USA
LVOW07s0034201217
560334LV00013B/1048/P

9 781988 297132